Complex Demonstratives

Contemporary Philosophical Monographs

Complex Demonstratives

A Quantificational Account

Jeffrey C. King

A Bradford Book

The MIT Press

Cambridge, Massachusetts

London, England

10024226804

This book was set in Sabon in '3B2' by Asco Typesetters, Hong Kong, and was printed and bound in the United States of America.

Library of Congress Cataloging-in-Publication Data

King, Jeffrey C.
  Complex demonstratives : a quantificational account / Jeffrey C. King.
     p.   cm. — (Contemporary philosophical monographs ; 2)
  "A Bradford book."
  Includes bibliographical references and index.
  ISBN 0-262-11263-9 (hc. : alk. paper) — ISBN 0-262-61169-4 (pbk. : alk. paper)
  1. Grammar, Comparative and general—Demonstratives. 2. Grammar, Comparative and general—Quantifiers. 3. Reference (Linguistics) I. Title. II. Series.
P299.D46 K56   2001
415—dc21   00-048174

T

For my mother, Eleanor Mae Smith King

Contents

Acknowledgments

The present work grew out of King (1999). Much of chapter 1 is drawn from that paper, as are parts of chapter 2. I thank *Noûs* and Blackwell Publishers for their kind permission to use this material. Many people have helped me think about the issues addressed herein. Early on, conversations with Kent Bach and David Sosa were very helpful to me. I presented an early version of King (1999) at U.C. Irvine, and Terry Parsons and Robert May made comments and suggestions that resulted in various improvements. A version of King (1999) was also presented at the Cornell Conference on Semantics and Pragmatics in March 1999, and I thank my commentator Mandy Simons and the conference participants for their discussion and comments. David Braun, David Kaplan, Ernie Lepore, Peter Ludlow, Kirk Ludwig, Ron Pritchard, Mark Richard, Mandy Simons, Jason Stanley, Zoltan Gendler Szabo, Mark Wilson, and the members of the Bay Area Philosophy of Language Discussion Group gave me useful help at one time or another as the present work developed. Material from the present work was presented at the InterAmerican Philosophy Congress in Puebla, Mexico in August 1999; to a graduate seminar at Cornell University in October 1999; and at the University of Pittsburgh in November 1999. I thank the audiences on those occasions for helpful discussions. The penultimate draft of this manuscript was completed during fall 1999. I spent this term of my sabbatical at Cornell University. Conversations with Jason Stanley and Zoltan Gendler Szabo during that term were extremely helpful and just plain fun. I should specifically mention the great debt I owe to Zoltan Gendler Szabo, who generously read an earlier version of the entire manuscript and provided comments that were an immense help in making revisions. In addition, I would like to thank three anonymous referees for MIT Press, who provided me with *very* insightful comments and suggestions that resulted in an improved manuscript. Thanks are also due to Ron Pritchard, who did a wonderful job of formatting, proofreading, producing the index, and helping to edit the final version of the manuscript. I was very fortunate to have worked with wonderful people from MIT Press on this project. In particular, Carolyn Gray Anderson, Judy Feldmann, and Peter Ludlow did their respective jobs perfectly, speedily, and with good humor. I enjoyed working with them and I thank them for their fine work. Finally, I mention the great intellectual debt I owe to the work of David Kaplan on this topic, particularly the wonderful Kaplan (1977). Though I ultimately disagree with many claims in this rich work, I, like many others, have learned an immense amount from it over the years.

Introduction

Since the seminal work of David Kaplan (1977), the ortho-
dox view of complex 'that' phrases (e.g., 'that man drinking a martini'—henceforth referred to as *'that' phrases*)
has been that they are contextually sensitive devices of
direct reference.[1] According to this view, the propositional
contribution of a 'that' phrase as it occurs in a context is
an individual. This individual is picked out by the *character*
of the 'that' phrase in question, where character is (or at
least is represented by) a function from context to content
or propositional contribution. The character of the 'that'
phrase in turn is determined by the demonstration or accompanying intention associated with the 'that' phrase,
together with the descriptive material combined with 'that'
to form the 'that' phrase.

Though there may be some disagreements concerning
the details of the proper direct reference story and though
there have been some recent challenges to this orthodoxy, I
think it is fair to say that most philosophers with any view
on the matter subscribe to the orthodoxy.[2]

The goal of the present work is to challenge this
orthodoxy. I shall show that direct reference accounts of
'that' phrases have real difficulties. I shall also show that
quantificational accounts can be formulated that not only
are as good as direct reference accounts on the data the

latter do best with, but go beyond direct reference accounts in handling a wider range of data than they do.

The plan of the monograph is as follows. In chapter 1, I lay out the arguments against direct reference accounts. Roughly speaking, these arguments fall into two categories. On the one hand, I cite uses of 'that' phrases that direct reference theorists apparently cannot handle (what I later call *NDNS uses*, *QI uses*, *NS readings* of certain sentences, and *Bach-Peters* type examples). And I claim that these uses suggest that a quantificational account of 'that' phrases is to be sought. On the other hand, I give syntactical arguments that 'that' phrases group with quantifier phrases rather than referring expressions when it comes to phenomena like antecedent contained deletion (ACD) and weak crossover effects. If they look like quantifiers, display weak crossover effects like quantifiers, behave like quantifiers in ACD constructions, then that is good reason to think they are quantifiers.

I begin chapter 2 by discussing what it is to be a quantificational theory of 'that' phrases. I then formulate three quantificational theories of 'that' phrases. I compare them in various ways and go on to argue in favor of one of the three. In so doing, I give the reader a fairly good feel for how this theory works.

In chapter 3, I apply the theory defended in chapter 2 to more complex data. In particular, I look at the interaction of 'that' phrases with modal operators, negation, and verbs of propositional attitude. If 'that' phrases are quantifiers, one would expect to find some evidence of scope interaction between 'that' phrases and other scoped elements. I argue here that there is such evidence.

Chapter 4 addresses a variety of issues that don't fit neatly with the issues addressed in other chapters, but which are significant and interesting. The issues addressed here include semantic properties of 'that' and other determiners; the possibility of extending our semantics for 'that' phrases to 'that' as a syntactically simple demonstrative; and a number of others.

Finally, chapter 5 argues against what I call *ambiguity approaches*. These are theories that hold that our various uses of 'that' phrases are not to be treated by a single semantical theory. They concede that I have shown that direct reference theories cannot handle all the uses of 'that' phrases I discuss. But they recommend holding onto direct reference theories for their favored uses and adopting some other account (perhaps even some version of the theory I defend) for the other uses. I argue that the theory I defend is superior to such an account.

The appendix contains a fairly simple, and in certain ways idealized, formal semantics.

Against Direct Reference Accounts

As mentioned in the introduction, the direct reference account of 'that' phrases, originally formulated by David Kaplan (1977), has the status of philosophical orthodoxy. Though I am concerned here to oppose this orthodoxy, I begin by noting a point of agreement with it. Throughout the present work, I shall assume that propositions are structured, sentence-like entities that have individuals, properties, and relations as constituents.[1] Thus, what is at issue here is the *nature of the contribution* made to propositions by 'that' phrases. Direct reference theorists claim that the contribution to a proposition made by a 'that' phrase (as it occurs in a context) is an individual. By contrast, I shall claim that 'that' phrases (as they occur in contexts) make contributions to propositions that are of the sort made by other quantificational noun phrases such as 'Every skier' and 'Most swimmers'. In chapter 2, I discuss what sorts of contributions quantificational noun phrases make to propositions, and hence what a quantificational account of 'that' phrases must say about the kind of contribution such phrases make to propositions. For now, it is enough that we recognize that what is at issue here is whether 'that' phrases contribute to propositions the sort of thing that referring expressions contribute to propositions, individuals, or the sort of thing that quantifiers contribute to propositions. With this in mind and before attempting to construct my alternative positive view, let me explain why direct reference accounts of 'that' phrases are problematic.

Those who espouse a directly referential semantics for 'that' phrases tend to focus on certain very particular uses of such phrases. They tend to consider only those uses in which a 'that' phrase is employed, along with a demonstration, to "talk about" something or someone in the (physical) context of utterance.[2] Though the direct reference account is plausible as applied to such uses, there are other uses of 'that' phrases for which the account seems problematic. In particular, I shall discuss three sorts of uses of 'that' phrases that direct reference accounts have problems with. I shall discuss two reasons for thinking that the first sort of use is problematic for direct reference theorists. A variety of strategies have been suggested to me that the direct reference theorist might employ to deal with the first reason for thinking that these uses are a problem for her. Thus, I shall describe the sort of use in question; explain the first reason I think it poses problems for the direct reference theorist; and consider strategies to which a direct reference theorist might appeal to get around the apparent problem and show why these strategies fail. I shall then discuss a further, perhaps more definitive reason for thinking direct reference theorists cannot handle the uses in question. Finally, I shall move on to two other uses that are more straightforwardly problematic for a direct reference account.

To begin with, then, there are uses of 'that' phrases in which they not accompanied by any demonstration, need not be used to talk about something present in the physical context of utterance, and in which the speaker has no particular individual in mind as "the thing she intends to talk about by means of the 'that' phrase." Suppose, for example, that Greg has just gotten back a math test on which he scored very poorly. Further, suppose that Greg knows on completely general grounds that exactly one student received a score of one hundred on the exam (e.g., suppose that Greg's evil but scrupulously honest teaching assistant told Greg this as he tossed Greg his failing effort). Reflecting on the difficulty of the exam, Greg says:

(1) That student who scored one hundred on the exam is a genius.

Let us call uses of this sort *no demonstration no speaker reference* uses, or *NDNS* uses for short. I take it that it is clear that the three conditions mentioned above are satisfied in the case as I have described it. Greg employs no demonstration, need not be talking about something present in the physical context of utterance (who knows where "the genius" is?), and has no one in mind as the individual he wants to talk about by means of the 'that' phrase.

Of course, nothing said to this point precludes holding that NDNS uses of 'that' phrases are directly referential. One could hold that the 'that' phrase in (1) contributes the individual satisfying the descriptive material attaching to 'that' to the proposition expressed by (1).[3] However, a further phenomenon involving NDNS uses is much harder for direct reference theorists to accommodate. Suppose that a classmate of Greg's hears Greg's teaching assistant tell Greg that exactly one student received one hundred on the exam, overhears Greg's (sincere) utterance of (1), and on that basis says to another of Greg's classmates:

(2) Greg believes that that student who scored one hundred on the exam is a genius

where the classmate's use of the 'that' phrase is itself an NDNS use.[4] The belief ascription seems clearly true in such a case. But how can the direct reference theorist explain this? According to the direct reference theorist, the embedded sentence in (2) expresses a singular proposition that has as a constituent the person the 'that' phrase in it refers to. So on this view, (2) asserts that Greg stands in the belief relation to this singular proposition. But it seems clear that Greg does not stand in the belief relation to the singular proposition in question. Greg, after all, appears to have only *general* beliefs and has no idea who scored one hundred percent on the examination. Thus it is hard to see how the direct reference theorist can explain the intuition that (2) is true in the situation described.

There are a number of maneuvers a direct reference theorist might make at this point to attempt to show that the intuition that (2) is true in the situation as described is not a problem for her. First, there is a strategy that would allow the direct reference theorist to say that Greg *does* stand in the belief relation to the singular proposition that she thinks is expressed by (1) and so hold that the belief ascription in (2) is true.[5] The direct reference theorist would note that Greg does possess a uniquely identifying description picking someone out in this case. Now according to the direct reference theorist, the 'that' phrase in (1) is directly referring. What Greg has done in uttering (1) is to introduce a term that directly refers to "the genius" by using the uniquely identifying description to fix the reference of the directly referential term. Having done this, Greg *does* stand in the belief relation to the singular proposition in question, and so (2), which according to the direct reference theorist asserts that Greg stands in the belief relation to the singular proposition in question, is literally true.

The underlying idea here is that whenever one has a uniquely identifying description, one can come to stand in the belief relation to singular propositions containing the individual satisfying the description by introducing a directly referential term whose reference is fixed by the description. I take it that the view is that to stand in the belief relation to a singular proposition in such a case, one must *actually introduce* a directly referential term whose reference is fixed by the description in question. It isn't enough merely to *possess* the uniquely identifying description. Otherwise, (assuming 'the *F*' has a denotation) there would never be a case in which a belief ascription containing a definite description 'the *F*' is true on the narrow scope reading of the description (where it ascribes a general belief to the effect that the *F* is *G*) and false on the wide scope reading (where it ascribes a belief in a singular proposition).

But then we can slightly alter our example so that the direct reference theorist cannot use this strategy to explain the intuition that (2) is true. Suppose that the situation regarding Greg is exactly as I described it previously except that instead of (1), Greg utters 'The student who scored one hundred percent on the exam is a genius'. Further suppose that Greg simply does not introduce a directly referential term (even in mentalese!) whose reference is fixed by his uniquely identifying description. Then even the direct reference theorist would have to hold that Greg believes only a general proposition in this case (the proposition expressed by the sentence 'The student who scored one hundred on the exam is a genius'). But if we imagine Greg's classmate uttering (2) in this situation (again, where the 'that' phrase has an NDNS use) we still have the intuition that (2) is true. And now the direct reference theorist has no explanation of this intuition! On the direct reference theorist's account, (2) asserts that Greg bears the belief relation to a singular proposition containing the student who received a score of one hundred on the exam. But in the case as described, Greg does *not* believe the singular proposition in question, and so (2) is false on the direct reference theorist's view. So the direct reference theorist cannot explain the intuition that (2) is true in *this* case as described. For the strategy under discussion, which she used to explain the intuition that (2) is true in the previous, slightly different case, is inapplicable here *even by her lights* as a result of Greg's failure to introduce any directly referring term that refers to the student who received a score of one hundred on the exam, and his thereby having only general beliefs.

The next move a direct reference theorist might make to avoid the claim that (2) causes her problems is to claim not to have the intuition that (2) is true in the *altered* version of the case just described.[6] To this, I can only say that I have found that informants who are not philosophers of language find (2)'s utterance straightforwardly and unproblematically true in such a situation. Perhaps the following story helps. Again, suppose that Greg was overheard by his friends sincerely saying 'The student who scored one hundred on the exam is a genius', where, again, he does not introduce a directly referential term (even in mentalese) whose reference is fixed by the uniquely satisfied description he employs. Later, a bunch of these friends of Greg's (who are aware that someone scored one hundred on the math exam but don't know who) are talking about Greg and some are claiming he never thinks anyone is highly intelligent. One friend, forgetting Greg's remarks about the student who scored one hundred, says, 'Yeah, Greg doesn't think *anyone* is a genius.' Another friend speaks up in Greg's defense, saying: 'That's not true. Greg believes that student who scored one hundred on the exam is a genius.' Surely, this remark will be taken as straightforwardly true by normal speakers in the situation as described.

Let's consider a final strategy for showing that (2) doesn't create problems for the direct reference theorist. We begin by agreeing that intuitively (2) is true in the (altered) situation as described. Assume as before that Greg was overheard by his friends sincerely saying 'The student who scored one hundred on the exam is a genius' (where he does not introduce a directly referential term, even in mentalese, whose reference is fixed by the uniquely satisfied description he employs). Suppose that, unbeknownst to Greg, Floyd is the student who scored one hundred on the exam (and that if asked specifically about *Floyd's* genius, Greg would sincerely say that he had no view on the matter). Still, the response continues, we have the intuition that the following is true in the situation as described:

(2a)   Greg believes Floyd is a genius.

But the fact that we are inclined to judge (2) *and* (2a) true in our situation shows that names and 'that' phrases behave in the same way here. Our "pattern of intuitions" is the same with proper names and 'that' phrases. Thus, assuming that names *are* directly referential, the intuition that (2) is true in the situation described cannot be evidence that the 'that' phrase in it does *not* directly refer. Of course, since the direct reference theorist (about names and 'that' phrases) must hold that (2) and (2a) are false in the situation described, she must give some explanation of our intuition that they are true. But one explanation will cover both cases; and she already needed and had an explanation of the intuitive truth of (2a) in the situation described.

The problem with this response on behalf of the direct reference theorist about 'that' phrases is that it overstates the extent to which names and 'that' phrases *do* behave the same way here. If we hold the facts about our altered situation constant (Floyd scored one hundred on the exam; Greg doesn't know this but says 'The student who scored one hundred on the exam is a genius'; Greg never introduces a directly referential term whose reference is fixed by the description 'the student who scored one hundred on the exam', etc.), perhaps in *some* contexts in which we

AGAINST DIRECT REFERENCE ACCOUNTS

imagine (2a) uttered we would have the intuition that it is true in our situation. For example, suppose Floyd is applying for a job and a question arises about his intelligence. We don't have any evidence either way, but we think Greg is good at judging genius based on performances on exams. Someone apprised of the facts tells us 'Well, Greg believes Floyd is a genius'. Intuitively, we might judge this remark true in this context. But now suppose that we have just asked Greg whether Floyd is a genius and he has sincerely responded (as we said he would) that he has no view on the matter. Greg leaves and someone walks in and says: 'You know, Greg believes that Floyd is a genius'. In this context, it seems to me, we have *no* inclination to regard the remark as true. So whether we have the intuition that (2a) is true in the situation as described depends on the context in which it is uttered and the relevant interests, etc., in that context. *But there is no such variation in our intuition that (2) is true in the situation as described*! Thus, contrary to what was claimed, our "pattern of intuitions" in the case is not the same with proper names and 'that' phrases. But then whatever explanation is given of our (varying) intuitions with respect to (2a) in the situation as described will not explain our (unvarying) intuitions with respect to (2) in the situation. So, again, the direct reference theorist has no explanation of our (unvarying) intuition that (2) is true in the situation as described. I would add that the fact that our intuition that (2) is true in our situation does *not* vary between contexts of utterance surely is strong prima facie evidence that (2) *is true* in the situation.

Thus, notwithstanding the direct reference theorist's above responses the 'that' phrase in (2) does after all appear to be problematic for her. But if the direct reference theorist cannot provide a satisfactory account of the use of the 'that' phrase in (2), there are grounds for thinking that she cannot provide an account of the 'that' phrase in (1) either. For the uses of 'that' phrases in both (1) and (2) are NDNS uses. It seems to me that we should expect a uniform semantic account of NDNS uses. Thus the failure of the direct reference account in the case of (2) militates in favor of rejecting such an account for the 'that' phrase in (1) as well. So in NDNS uses of 'that' phrases we have data that is problematic for the direct reference theorist.

As mentioned above, there is a second and even more definitive reason for thinking that NDNS uses are not directly referential. This can be seen more clearly by considering a slightly different example. Suppose that Scott the scientist is lecturing his class on great moments in hominid history. He is discussing various hominid discoveries and inventions, and the intelligence they required. He has just introduced the topic of the discovery of how to start fires. He says:

(3)   That hominid who discovered how to start fires was a genius.

Scott's use of the 'that' phrase here is clearly an NDNS use. He employs no demonstration, obviously has no particular individual "in mind" as the individual he intends to talk about, and certainly is not talking about any creature in the physical context of his utterance. Consider the proposition expressed by (3) as uttered by Scott in the actual world. Suppose that in the actual world, Homey the hominid discovered how to start fires and Homey was indeed a brilliant hominid (so presumably on all accounts of the semantics of 'that' phrases, the proposition expressed by (3) is true in the actual world). Now consider a possible world w' in which Homey was a genius but was not the hominid to discover how to start fires. In w', this discovery was made by Shomey the hominid, who was a feeble-minded, bumbling hominid and simply got lucky. Now is the proposition Scott expressed by uttering (3) (in the actual world) true or false in this circumstance? It seems clear that it is false. But if the 'that' phrase in (3) were rigid, it would denote Homey in w' and the proposition expressed by (3) would be true![7] Hence the 'that' phrase is nonrigid. Of course, the fact that NDNS uses such as this are nonrigid precludes treating them as directly referential.

A second sort of use of 'that' phrases that causes serious problems for a direct reference treatment is illustrated by the following examples:

(4) Every father dreads that moment when his oldest child leaves home.

(5) Most avid snow skiers remember that first black diamond run they attempted to ski.

Both (4) and (5) have readings on which the 'that' phrases contain pronouns that function as variables bound by quantifiers in whose scope the 'that' phrases occur.[8] Let us call such uses *quantification in* uses, or *QI* uses for short. Clearly, QI uses of 'that' phrases such as those in (4) and (5) don't refer, let alone directly refer, to particular individuals.

There is another use of 'that' phrases, closely related to QI uses, that poses problems for the direct reference theorist. Consider the following sentences:

(6) That professor who brought in the biggest grant in each division will be honored.

(7) That senator with the most seniority on each committee is to be consulted.

Both (6) and (7) are ambiguous. The ambiguity of (6) can be brought out by different continuations. First, imagine it followed by: 'Her name is Cini Brown and she is a fine researcher.' On this reading, the 'that' phrase is being used to talk about a particular individual, and so the direct reference theorist can account for the reading. But now imagine the following continuation: 'In all ten professors will be honored'. Let us call this reading of (6) the *narrow scope (NS) reading*.[9] The existence of NS readings of (6) and (7) seems hard to reconcile with the claim that 'that' phrases are directly referential. For on these readings, the 'that' phrases are not referring to any particular individuals. Intuitively, in (6) the 'that' phrase is used to make a claim about the professors who brought in the most grant money in different divisions. So again here, the direct reference theorist is in trouble.

In summary, we have found three sorts of cases in which 'that' phrases do not seem to be functioning as directly referential terms. It is worth noting that all three cases suggest some sort of quantificational treatment. Without attempting to be specific about the exact nature of the quantification that might be involved and so thinking that the 'that' phrases in such cases may be functioning something like the way in which definite descriptions, understood as quantifier phrases, function, we can get some handle on the NDNS and QI uses, as well as the NS readings of (6) and (7). In the case of NDNS uses, if the 'that' phrase contributes to the proposition expressed some complex descriptive condition that must be (uniquely) satisfied for the proposition to be true, we can see that a speaker could express a proposition using a sentence containing such a phrase when no demonstration is involved and the speaker had no one in mind (as in (1) in the situation described). More important, one can see how a belief ascription like (2) could be true in the situation described. For the ascription would assert that Greg believes a proposition containing a descriptive condition instead of an individual, as the direct reference theorist would have it. And of course if the complex descriptive condition (at least in some cases) could "determine" different individuals in different circumstances of evaluation, this would allow the 'that' phrases in (1)–(3) to be nonrigid. As for the QI uses in (4) and (5), we would have one quantifier phrase binding variables in another, as happens in many other cases, for example:

(8a)   Every man loves some woman he kissed.

(8b)   Every woman loves the man she first kissed.

And finally, if 'that' phrases are quantifiers, we would expect scope interactions between 'that' phrases and other quantifiers. Thus the two readings of (6) and (7) are a result of a scope ambiguity, and we explain the NS readings as resulting from the 'that' phrases taking narrow scope relative to the quantifier phrases occurring in their relative clauses. Thus QI uses, NDNS uses, and the NS readings of (6) and (7) suggest *both* that a direct reference account is incorrect *and* that a quantificational account is to be sought.

There are a number of additional arguments for the claim that 'that' phrases are quantificational and not directly referential. First, consider Bach-Peters sentences such as the following:

(9)   Every friend of yours who studied for it passed some math exam she was dreading,

where the pronoun in each noun phrase ('it' in 'Every friend of yours who studied for it' and 'she' in 'some math exam she was dreading') is interpreted as anaphoric on the other noun phrase. The most plausible explanations of the acceptability and semantics of such sentences assume that the phrases containing the anaphoric pronouns are both quantifier phrases. Note that sentences like (9), with pronouns understood anaphorically, can be formed using virtually any quantifier phrases:

(10a)   Few friends of yours who studied for them passed several exams they were dreading.

(10b)   Most friends of yours who studied for them passed many exams they were dreading.

(10c)   No friends of yours who studied for them passed at least two exams they were dreading.

Acceptable sentences exactly like (9) and (10a)–(10c) can be formed using 'that' phrases:

(11)   That friend of yours who studied for it passed that math exam she was dreading.

As with (9) and (10a)–(10c), this sentence is acceptable with the pronouns interpreted anaphorically. If we suppose that the 'that' phrases are quantifier phrases, the explanation of the acceptability and semantics of (9) and (10a)–(10c) can be carried straight over to (11). That the data comprising (9), (10a)–(10c), and (11) is to be subsumed under a single explanation is made even more plausible by the fact that we can get sentences of this sort in which 'that' phrases combine with other quantifier phrases:

(11a)   Every friend of yours who studied for it passed that exam she was dreading.

(11b)   That friend of yours who studied for it passed some math exam she was dreading.

To summarize, explanations of the acceptability and semantics of (9) and (10a)–(10c), where the pronouns are understood as anaphoric, are necessary and available. Such explanations assume that the noun phrases in those sentences are quantifiers. On the hypothesis that 'that' phrases are quantifier phrases, (11), (11a), and (11b) are automatically subsumed under these very explanations.

By contrast, (11) and (11a) are quite puzzling on the hypothesis that 'that' phrases are devices of direct reference. Taking (11) first, if we assume that the 'that' phrases are directly referential, the pronouns anaphoric on them apparently must be taken to refer to the same thing as their antecedents. Thus, the anaphoric pronouns are referring expressions that inherit their referents from their antecedents. But this leads directly to problems. On a direct reference view, the predicative material that combines with 'that' to form a 'that' phrase partly determines the character, and hence the referent in the context of utterance, of the 'that' phrase.[10] But then, the character of the 'that' phrase will be partly determined by the referents of any referring expressions occurring in the predicative material that partly comprises the 'that' phrase. Thus, for example, the character, and hence the referent in a context, of 'that guy standing next to Mark' will be partly determined by the referent of 'Mark'. But now consider 'That friend of yours who studied for it' in (11). Its character, and hence referent in a context, depends in part on the referent of 'it'. And the referent of 'it' is determined by its antecedent 'that math exam she was dreading'. Thus the determination of a character, and hence a referent in a context, for 'That friend of yours who studied for it' requires having secured a referent for 'it', which in turn requires having secured a character, and hence referent in a context, for its antecedent 'that math exam she was dreading'. But the character of 'that math exam she was dreading' is partly determined by the referent of 'she'. And the referent of 'she' is inherited from 'That friend of your who studied for it'. Thus 'That friend of yours who studied for it' must be assigned a character, and hence a referent in a context, in order that 'she' be assigned a referent. But, as we have seen, this cannot be done until a referent is secured for 'it'! The upshot is that it is hard to see how the character of either 'that' phrase in (11) can be determined. The determination of the character of a given 'that' phrase in (11) requires securing a referent for the pronoun in it. This in turn requires securing a referent and hence a character for the other 'that' phrase. But this requires securing a referent for the pronoun in *it*, which presupposes a referent and hence a character for the other 'that' phrase. The bottom line is that determining the character of either 'that' phrase presupposes having determined the character of the other. Thus neither can be assigned a character, nor, therefore, a referent. So it is hard to see how a direct reference theory can explain the acceptability, and, in the appropriate circumstances, the truth, of (11).[11]

(11a) only exacerbates the direct reference theorist's problem. For (11a) has a reading on which it asserts that every friend passed that exam she was dreading, possibly different exams for different friends (compare: 'Every employee who worked for it received that promotion she had hoped for'). But since on this reading the 'that' phrase is used to talk about the various exams passed by each friend, it can hardly be a referring term. Thus, even if the direct reference theorist were to figure out some way to handle (11) on the assumption that the 'that' phrases in it directly refer, it seems certain that the account would fail to handle (11a). So it appears unlikely in the extreme that the direct reference theorist can give a unified account of (11) and (11a).

In summary, each of (11) and (11a) taken separately is quite problematic for the direct reference theorist. And it appears that in any case she cannot give a unified account of them. By contrast, the view that 'that' phrases are quantifiers can appeal directly to already existing explanations for (9) and (10a)–(10c) in explaining both (11) and (11a) (and (11b)). Thus, not only does such a view give a unified account of (11)–(11b), but it places them among the broader array of similar data represented by (9) and (10a)–(10c). Surely, this is the much more theoretically satisfying account of (11)–(11b).

AGAINST DIRECT REFERENCE ACCOUNTS

There are additional reasons for thinking that 'that' phrases are quantificational, which have to do with their syntactical behavior. On one widely held view of syntax, there is a level of syntactic representation whose representations are phrase structure representations (represented by trees or bracketings labeled with linguistic categories) derived from surface structure by means of transformations, and whose representations are interpreted by the semantic component.[12] This level of syntactic representation is called *LF* (for *logical form*). According to such views (or at least prominent versions of such views), one of the primary differences between LF representations and surface structure (or S-structure) representations is that in the mapping to LF, quantifier phrases get "moved" and end up binding variables (called *traces*) at the level of LF. To illustrate, consider the following S-structure:

(12) $[_s[_{np}$Every skier] $[_{vp}$is happy]]

In the mapping of this S-structure representation to LF, the quantifier phrase gets adjoined to the (S) node leaving behind a trace (e_1) that functions as a bound variable:

(13) $[_s[_{np}$Every skier]$_1$ $[_s e_1$ $[_{vp}$is happy]]]

For a sentence containing two or more quantifier phrases, this movement results in explicit representation of relative quantifier scope at the level of LF. Thus an S-structure such as

(14) $[_s[_{np}$Every philosopher] $[_{vp}$hates $[_{np}$some new age flake]]]

has two LF representations, resulting from the fact that the rules mapping S-structure to LF may apply in two different ways:

(15) $[_s[_{np}$every philosopher]$_1$ $[_s[_{np}$some new age flake]$_2$ $[_s e_1$ hates e_2]]]

(16) $[_s[_{np}$some new age flake$]_2$ $[_s[_{np}$every philosopher$]_1$ $[_se_1$ hates $e_2]]]$

The quantifier scope ambiguity of (14) is thus explained by the fact that (15) and (16) are interpreted differently by the semantic component.

For our purposes, the important point in all of this is that on such approaches to syntax, quantifier phrases and singular referring terms (such as names) are treated differently in the mapping from S-structure to LF. Quantifiers undergo "movement" of the sort just described, whereas referring expressions do not. This being so, whether an expression undergoes movement in the mapping to LF indicates whether it is a quantifier or not.[13]

There are certain constructions that can be used to detect this sort of movement. First, it appears to be a condition on verb phrase (VP) deletion that neither the missing verb nor its antecedent c-commands the other.[14] Yet a variety of examples appear to violate this condition. In examples like

(17) Tiger birdied every hole that Michael did

'birdied' c-commands 'did'.[15] However, though this is so at S-structure, if it is assumed that quantifier phrases are moved, resulting in their being adjoined to the S node at LF (leaving behind traces), 'birdied' will not c-command 'did' at LF as a result of the movement of 'every hole that Michael did'. Thus, if we assume that the constraint on VP deletion is a constraint that must be satisfied only at the level of LF and that quantifier phrases are moved in the way suggested in the mapping to LF, examples like (17) don't constitute counterexamples to what appears to be an otherwise well-motivated constraint on VP deletion. If all of this is correct, then the acceptability of

(18) Tiger birdied that hole that Michael did

suggests that 'that' phrases are moved in the mapping to LF and so are quantifier phrases. Thus we have some syntactic evidence that 'that' phrase are quantificational.[16]

Further, so-called weak crossover phenomena also appear to support the view that 'that' phrases are quantificational, and so provide more syntactic evidence in favor of this view. The following sentence has no interpretation on which 'his' is anaphoric on 'every man' (i.e., no reading on which it means that every man is loved by his mother):

(19)   His mother loves every man.

If we form sentences using quantifier phrases other than 'every man', again we never get sentences in which the pronoun can be interpreted as anaphoric on the quantifier:

(19a)   His mother loves some man.

(19b)   His mother loves the man with the goatee.

(19c)   His mother loves no man.

(19d)   Their mothers love few men.

(19e)   Their mothers love several men.

By contrast, if we replace the quantifier phrase with a name, we are able to interpret the pronoun as anaphoric on the name. Thus the following sentence has a reading on which it means that John's mother loves him:

(19′)   His mother loves John.

To some extent, different theorists explain the weak crossover effects exhibited in (19)–(19e) differently. However, it is generally held that the explanation as to why one cannot get anaphoric readings in (19)–(19e) and sentences like them must make essential reference to the fact that a quantifier phrase occurs in object position and, unlike a name, undergoes movement in the mapping to LF.[17] After all, when this is not so, as in (19′), we can get the anaphoric readings.

That quantifier phrases and referring expressions behave differently in such constructions is made even more plausible by noting that when we substitute a deictic referring expression for the name 'John' in (19′), we can read the sentence-initial pronoun as anaphoric on the deictic referring expression. Thus, imagine I am in a room with a number of people and the question comes up of who is loved by his mother. I utter the following, pointing only when I say 'him':

(19′a)   Well, his mother loves [pointing] him.[18]

Thus whatever the precise mechanism, it appears that in such examples, quantifier phrases exhibit weak crossover effects ((19)–(19e)) and referring expressions do not ((19′)–(19′a)). And as the following example illustrates, 'that' phrases, like (other) quantifier phrases, *do* exhibit weak crossover effects:

(19″)   His mother loves that man with the goatee.

It seems clear to me that the pronoun 'his' cannot be interpreted as anaphoric on 'that man with the goatee'.[19] Surely it is striking and suggestive that 'that' phrases cluster with quantifier phrases and not with referring expressions with respect to weak crossover effects. So again here we have some syntactic evidence that 'that' phrases are quantificational and not directly referential.[20]

There is a final point, implicit in what has been argued so far, that I wish to emphasize. As I have indicated, it would appear that the direct reference theorist must hold that in NDNS uses, it is the descriptive material combined with 'that' in the 'that' phrase that *alone* determines the character of the 'that' phrase, demonstrations and the sorts of intentions that accompany them being absent in such cases. On the other hand, it would appear that the best hope the direct reference theorist has of accounting for Bach-Peters sentences like (11), when used with accompanying demonstrations, is to hold that in such cases the predicative material combined with 'that' in the 'that' phrase plays *no* role in the determination of character. For if this were so, the determination of the character of the 'that' phrases would not require a prior determination of referents for the pronouns, and so the vicious circularity in the determination of character we noted would be avoided. Thus, to handle both NDNS and Bach-Peters cases, the direct reference theorist's best move appears to be to claim that sometimes predicative material in 'that' phrases plays *no* role in character determination (Bach-Peters sentences) and sometimes it *alone* determines character (NDNS cases). Of course such an account sounds quite ad hoc. But there is a much worse problem. There are Bach-Peters sentences in which the 'that' phrases have NDNS uses, for example, (11) uttered in a situation in which the speaker knows on general grounds that her addressee has a unique friend who studied for, dreaded, and passed a unique math exam. It is utterly unclear what the direct reference theorist is to say here. It would appear that she *must* hold that the predicative material determines the character of the 'that' phrases in such cases. But this leads directly to our vicious circularity in the determination of character.

A similar problem arises with respect to QI uses of a sort that the direct reference theorist *might* have hoped to be able to handle. I wish to stress that QI uses such as (4) and (5) just seem hopeless on a direct reference account; but the direct reference theorist *might* have hoped to be able to handle *certain* examples. Suppose I and my audience have been told that some senator from New York (we don't know who) had his unique mistress (we don't know whom) appointed ambassador to Rongovia. Reminding my friends of how corrupt government officials are, I say

(20)   As we all clearly recall, some senator from New York had that mistress of his appointed ambassador to Rongovia.

Here again, no demonstrations or the sorts of intentions that accompany them are present. Thus, the direct reference theorist must hold that the predicative material 'mistress of his' alone determines the character of the 'that' phrase. But it is hard to see how this could be. For character determination is supposed to occur "prepropositionally," and is part of the explanation as to why a given sentence expresses a given proposition. However, because the pronoun 'his' is anaphoric on and apparently bound by 'some senator', it will not be assigned any value prepropositionally. Presumably, the pronoun (or its propositional contribution) will come into play semantically only when the quantifier binding it (or its propositional contribution) is processed. But then how could 'mistress of his' *prepropositionally* determine a character that suffices to uniquely determine a referent in the context in question?

Thus NDNS Bach-Peters examples and QI uses like (20) in the situation as described show that even a direct reference theory that tried to handle (at best) some of our data by allowing the roles of predicative material and demonstrations in character determination to vary from cases to case will fail.

Let us summarize our discussion to this point. First, we noted that certain uses of 'that' phrases, specifically QI uses, NDNS uses, and the NS readings of (6) and (7), are hard to account for on the hypothesis that 'that' phrases are directly referential. Second, we noted that an account of such uses according to which the 'that' phrases are quantifier phrases seemed promising. Third, we adduced a number of additional reasons, involving Bach-Peters sentences, VP deletion, and weak crossover phenomena, for holding that 'that' phrases are quantifier phrases. Finally, we showed that even if the direct reference theorist allows predicative material and demonstrations to play different roles in character determination in different cases, she will still run into problems.

It is time to look for an account of 'that' phrases that can handle *all* the data we have discussed.

Three Quantificational Accounts of 'That'

Phrases

In the previous chapter, we saw that there are good reasons for thinking that 'that' phrases are not directly referential but quantificational. We now face the task of constructing a quantificational account of 'that' phrases.

In fact, as discussed below, I shall construct three different quantificational accounts of 'that' phrases. However, before getting to this, it is important to discuss what *any* quantificational account of 'that' phrases would have to be like (i.e., what it is to *be* a quantificational account of 'that' phrases). Next, I shall discuss a common feature of all three quantificational accounts that we shall consider. Following this, I turn to the construction of the three quantificational accounts. The first is an account I defended in previous work.[1] Having sketched this account, I shall explain why I no longer favor it. I shall then describe two other quantificational accounts and compare their treatments of a variety of data. After providing reasons for favoring one of these two accounts, I shall go on to discuss how it treats additional data.

With these preliminary remarks out of the way, let us now turn to the task of saying what it is to be a quantificational account of 'that' phrases. Standard quantifier phrases such as 'Most skiers', 'No Californian with any sense', and 'Few people who grew up in Dryden' are syntactically complex noun phrases (NP or N''). They result from combining *determiners* ('every', 'some', 'most', 'the', etc.) with syntactically simple or complex N' constituents ('man', 'woman who is smart', 'friends of Scott's from Illinois').[2] There are a number of ways to handle natural language quantification within a theory of structured propositions of the sort I am presupposing here. On the approach I favor, determiners such as 'some', 'every', 'few', 'the', and so on contribute two-place relations between properties to propositions.[3] Thus 'some' contributes to propositions the relation between properties of *having a common instance*. 'Every' contributes to propositions the relation that obtains between the properties A and B iff every instance of A is an instance of B. 'Few' contributes to propositions the relation that obtains between properties A and B iff few instances of A are instances of B, and so on.

The idea, then, in broad outline, is that a sentence of the form

(1)   Det N_1 is/are N_2

(where Det is a determiner, N_1 is a simple or complex N' constituent, and N_2 is a predicate nominal or adjective; and where, again, N_1 and N_2 agree with the syntactic number of Det) expresses a proposition to which Det contributes a two-place relation R between properties, and to which N_1 and N_2 both contribute properties, say N_{1^*} and N_{2^*}, respectively.[4] Thus (1) expresses a proposition that looks something like

(1a) $[[R[N_{1^*}]]N_{2^*}]$.

(1a) is true (at a world w) iff N_{1^*} stands in the relation R to N_{2^*} (at w). Thus a sentence such as 'Every woman is smart' expresses a proposition that is true at w iff in w the property expressed by 'woman' stands in the relation expressed by 'every' to the property expressed by 'smart' (i.e., iff in *w* every instance of the property of being a woman is an instance of the property of being smart).[5] This approach is easily generalized to examples involving VPs not containing the copula. But we need not delve into this at present.

A quantificational account of 'that' phrases ought to claim that 'that' is a determiner just as 'some', 'few', 'every', and 'the' are, and so combines with an N' constituent to yield an NP. On the semantic side, 'that', like the other determiners, presumably contributes to propositions a two-place relation between properties. Of course, in formulating a quantificational account of 'that' phrases, one might well claim, as I will, that 'that' phrases are importantly different from standard quantifier phrases like 'every woman'. For one thing, 'that' phrases seem to exhibit a sort of contextual sensitivity not exhibited by standard quantifier phrases. Still, if one denies that 'that' contributes to propositions a relation of the same category (i.e., a two-place relation between properties) as other determiners do, one will end up claiming that 'that' phrases (and/or their syntactic constituents) really are *extremely* different from ordinary quantifier phrases, either syntactically or semantically or both.[6] Of course, a quantificational theorist about 'that' phrases might be *forced* to such a view. But it seems to me that in defending a quantificational account of 'that' phrases, it would be desirable to hold that they function as much like other quantifier phrases as possible. After all, it is, if nothing else, a bit misleading to claim that one is defending the view that 'that' phrases are quantificational only to defend a view according to which they are syntactically or semantically wildly different from other quantifiers. Thus, within the quantificational framework I am making use of, I henceforth shall take it as a constraint on a quantificational account of 'that' phrases that it holds that 'that' is a determiner and so contributes a two-place relation between properties to propositions, as other determiners do.

I wish to emphasize that in what is to come I am not merely claiming that 'that' phrases *may* be treated as quantificational. This claim, after all, is almost trivial. Since the work of Montague, it has been known that one can treat all noun phrases, including proper names, as quantifiers in the sense that one can find a sort of semantic value that is appropriate for quantified noun phrases and assign semantic values of the same sort to names. In the usual (extensional) generalized quantifier framework, for example, one assigns to quantifier phrases sets of sets of individuals. Thus a sentence like 'Every man is happy' is true iff the set of individuals assigned to 'happy' (i.e., the set of happy individuals) is a member of the set of sets of individuals assigned to 'every man' (i.e., the set of sets S of individuals such that every man is in S). One could, of course, assign a name 'Alice' a set of sets of individuals as well (i.e., the set of sets S of individuals that contain Alice). Thus, 'Alice is happy' is true iff the set assigned to 'happy' (i.e., the set of happy individuals) is a member of the set of sets assigned 'Alice'. In this way, proper names have the same sorts of denotations as quantifier phrases.[7] But clearly, if one were to claim on this basis that names are quantifiers, one would be making a fairly uninteresting claim. To claim similarly that 'that' phrases *could* be treated as quantificational is equally insipid.

But the force of the arguments of chapter 1 is that we *must* treat 'that' phrases as quantificational. I argued there that treating them as contextually sensitive referring expressions fails. And the latter is the most promising, prominent, and plausible nonquantificational account. Further, we saw that the data that militated against such a treatment strongly suggested a quantificational account of 'that' phrases. We also saw that there is syntactic evidence that 'that' phrases are quantificational. A comparable argument could not be given for the case of names—or rather, if it could be, to claim on that basis that names are quantificational would hardly be insipid.

With these remarks in place, let us begin to discuss quantificational accounts of 'that' phrases by addressing an issue that is resolved in the same way on all three of the quantificational accounts I shall sketch.

Direct reference theorists hold, and in fact I agree, that demonstrations or the intentions accompanying them are relevant to the semantics of 'that' phrases. One reason for thinking this has to do with the explanation of differences between the behavior of 'that' phrases and definite descriptions. I assume that though speaker's intentions and demonstrations sometimes accompany uses of definite descriptions, they are of no semantic significance when accompanying definite descriptions. (Both Russell's account and current accounts, such as Neale [1990], of the semantics of definite descriptions endorse this claim.) If this is so, then one semantic difference between definite descriptions and 'that' phrases is that demonstrations or speaker's intentions have a semantic role when accompanying the latter but not when accompanying the former. This difference, it seems to me, explains why the phrase 'that F' can be used several times in a situation in which there are many Fs to talk about distinct Fs, whereas 'the F' often cannot be. For example, looking at cars in a lot filled with new cars, one can say 'That car is nicer than that car', talking about distinct cars by means of the distinct occurrences of 'that car'. However, one could not felicitously use 'the' phrases instead: 'The car is nicer than the car' (with or without accompanying demonstrations) is infelicitous. If demonstrations or speaker intentions are relevant to the semantics of 'that' phrases, different demonstrations or intentions associated with the distinct occurrences of 'that *F*' would allow them to be used to talk about distinct *F*s, which would explain the felicity of 'That car is nicer than that car'. By contrast, the semantics of 'the' does not allow a role for demonstrations or speaker intentions. Thus, there is nothing that allows the distinct occurrences of 'the *F*' to be used to talk about different *F*s. Hence the attempt to use distinct occurrences of 'the *F*' to talk about distinct *F*s in an *F*-filled environment results in infelicity.[8]

Of course, direct reference theorists hold that demonstrations or the intentions accompanying them are relevant to the semantics of 'that' phrases by partly determining the *characters*, and hence the referents in contexts, of 'that' phrases. However, since on a quantificational account 'that' phrases are not referring expressions, such an account cannot hold that demonstrations or accompanying intentions are relevant in the way direct reference theorists claim they are. Thus I need to explain how, on any quantificational account of 'that' phrases, demonstrations or accompanying intentions are relevant to their semantics.

In the first place, let me make clear that I hold that it is the *intentions* speakers have in using 'that' phrases, and not the demonstrations that are manifestations of those intentions, that are relevant to the semantics of 'that' phrases.[9] Further, I claim that speakers have at least three kinds of intentions when they use 'that' phrases in the various ways described earlier, at least two of which are importantly different. I shall begin by discussing these three kinds of intentions. To anticipate what is to come, I shall claim that all three kinds of intentions uniquely determine properties, which then figure in the semantics of 'that' phrases. Again I stress that making intentions relevant to the semantics of 'that' phrases in the way discussed below is a common feature of all the quantificational accounts of 'that' phrases I shall discuss.[10]

The first sort of intention occurs in cases of the sort that direct reference theorists have primarily concentrated on. In such a case, the speaker is perceiving something in her physical environment and has an intention to talk about it. I shall say in such a case that the speaker has a *perceptual intention*. I do not intend to say exactly what it is to have a perceptual intention; presumably it is a matter of being in certain psychological and perceptual states, where the thing one intends to talk about bears the appropriate sorts of relations (causal and whatever else) to those states. In such a case, let us say that the thing one intends to talk about is *the object of the perceptual intention in question*. Thus the intention, taken in the broad sense as including the relevant perceptual and psychological states of the person as well as the object of the intention and the relations between these in virtue of which the object is the object of the intention, uniquely determines at least two properties, both of which are possessed uniquely by the object of the intention. First, the object of the intention possesses a certain relational property: the property of bearing certain relations to the relevant perceptual and psychological states of the person with the perceptual intention, in virtue of which the object of the intention is the object of the intention. Let us call this relational property the property of *being the object of the perceptual intention in question*. Second, assuming that b is the object of the intention in question, the intention uniquely determines the property of *being identical to b*.

The second sort of intention is closely related to the first. This sort of intention occurs in cases in which, having perceived something in the past, a speaker forms a current intention to talk about that thing. For example, a speaker may have observed a man kissing Elizabeth last night, and forms a current intention to talk about him. In such a case, I will say that the speaker has a *past perceptual intention*.

As in the previous case, I don't intend to say precisely what it is to have a past perceptual intention. Presumably it is a matter of currently being in certain psychological states and having been in certain perceptual states, where the thing one intends to talk about bears the appropriate sorts of relations (causal and whatever else) to those states. In such a case, let us again say that the thing one intends to talk about is *the object of the past perceptual intention in question*. Thus, a given past perceptual intention uniquely determines at least two properties, as in the previous case, both of which are uniquely possessed by the object of the intention. First, there is the relational property of bearing certain relations to the relevant past perceptual and current psychological states of the person with the past perceptual intention, in virtue of which the object of the intention is the object of the intention. Second, assuming the object of the intention is b, the intention uniquely determines the property of *being identical to b*. Because this case is so similar to the previous one, I shall in general speak of only perceptual intentions, concentrating on the first case and supposing that these cases will be handled in a very similar way.

The third sort of intention is importantly different from the previous two and occurs when a speaker believes that something uniquely possesses certain properties and intends to say something about the thing with those properties. So, for example, Danielle sees a poster that says (correctly) that someone (whose name she couldn't quite make out) will be swimming across Lake Tahoe starting at noon the next day. The following day at 12:15 P.M. Danielle has the intention to say something about the person who is currently swimming across Tahoe. Let us call such an intention a *descriptive intention*. Given a descriptive intention, there is a property or conjunction of properties C such that the speaker intends to say something about whatever possesses C. We shall call this property or conjunction of properties *the property of the descriptive intention in question*. Thus, once again, the intention uniquely determines a property.

As we shall see, speakers' intentions in these three cases determine other properties as well, but these are best discussed after more preliminaries.

Having discussed these three sorts of intentions and certain properties they determine, let us return to the semantics of 'that' phrases. Earlier I said that any quantificational account of 'that' phrases must hold that 'that' contributes to propositions a two-place relation between properties. I also said that the properties determined by speakers' intentions in using 'that' phrases lately discussed will figure in the semantics of 'that' phrases.

The most natural and straightforward way of fitting these two ideas together is to hold that although 'that', as used in a given context, contributes a two-place relation between properties to propositions just as other determiners do, 'that', taken "outside of any context," expresses a relation with some number of additional argument places. The idea is that when a speaker uses a 'that' phrase in a particular context, his intentions determine properties that saturate these additional argument places in the relation expressed by 'that'. The result of this saturation is a *two*-place relation between properties. This two-place relation between properties is then contributed to the proposition expressed in that context by the sentence containing the 'that' phrase. So though 'that' taken out of any context expresses a relation with more than two places, as used in a context it always ends up contributing a two-place relation between properties to propositions, just as other determiners do. I claim that in this way we can capture the various semantic features of 'that' phrases, including their contextual sensitivity.

It is perhaps worth remarking that talk of 'that' "taken outside of any context" expressing a relation with more than two places is to be understood as making a claim about the lexical meaning of 'that' qua determiner. Its lexical meaning is a more-than-two-place relation. When speakers use it in a context, all but two argument places in the relation that is its lexical meaning are saturated by properties determined by the intentions of the speakers in the context. Thus, on this view, the more-than-two-place relation that is the meaning of 'that' determines a function from properties (determined by the speaker's intentions) to two-place relations between properties (that 'that' as used in a context contributes to the proposition expressed in that context by the sentence in which it occurs).

In providing a specific quantificational account of 'that' phrases we must describe the more-than-two-place relation expressed outside of any context by 'that' (i.e., the lexical meaning of 'that'); describe which properties determined by a speaker's intentions saturate argument places in that relation; and describe the resulting two-place relation between properties 'that' as used in a context contributes to a proposition. We face a number of choices here, with different theories resulting from those choices. Because I would like to give the reader some sense of the range of available theories, as well as ultimately defend one of them, I shall discuss *some* of the ways in which quantificational theories of 'that' phrases can vary. In particular, as already mentioned, I shall formulate three quantificational accounts and discuss what I view as their pros and cons. In the end, I shall claim that one of these theories is the best.

It should be emphasized that we have already made one choice that has reduced the range of possible theories. In claiming that it is intentions, and not the demonstrations that are their manifestations, that are relevant to the semantics of 'that' phrases, and further that these intentions uniquely determine the properties previously described, we have already ruled out certain theories. For one might have claimed that it is the *demonstrations* that are relevant and that they determine *different* properties from those determined by intentions. Or there may be *other* properties uniquely determined by intentions that we have not discussed. Or perhaps demonstrations or accompanying intentions could be worked into the semantics in some utterly different way. Again, I simply mention these possibilities to give the reader the sense of the available theoretical space.

Given the choices we have made to this point, the main ways that quantificational theories can vary are the following. Theories can differ with respect to the number of argument places had by the relation that 'that' expresses outside of any context and with respect to what this relation is; and they can differ with respect to what properties or other entities saturate argument places in this relation, yielding the two-place relation between properties 'that' (as used in a context) contributes to propositions. Thus, even here, there are many theories. The three theories I shall sketch will serve to illustrate how theories can differ in the ways just mentioned.

I shall begin with the theory I defended in previous work.[11] On this theory the lexical meaning of 'that' ("what it expresses outside of any context") is a four-place relation, three of whose places are appropriate for properties (the "nonproperty" argument place will be discussed shortly). I initiate the discussion of this theory by highlighting a feature of it shared by the other two theories I shall discuss. As mentioned above in discussing speakers' intentions, they determine a property P^*, which then saturates one of the property argument places in the relation expressed by 'that'. On the present theory, we begin with a four-place relation, three of whose argument places are property argument places. So the result of this saturation is a three-place relation, two of whose argument places are appropriate for properties.

On all three theories I intend to discuss, this particular saturation has the same semantic effect. The way to think of this intuitively is that the semantics of 'that' allows speakers' intentions to supplement the predicative material combined with 'that' to yield a quantifier phrase. That is, the predicative material combined with 'that' to form a quantifier phrase *restricts* the quantification: combining 'that' with 'guy wearing blue pants' restricts the quantification to guys wearing blue pants, since 'guy wearing blue pants' expresses the property of being a guy wearing blue pants. This restriction can be supplemented by a property determined by the speaker's intentions so that the quantification is restricted to guys wearing blue pants *and possessing the property determined by the speaker's intention.* Again, let me emphasize that the idea that speakers' intentions determine properties that further restrict the quantification expressed by a use of a 'that' phrase is common to all the theories I am going to discuss.[12]

In the limiting case, speakers' intentions will have no semantic effect. Imagine an instance of our second case above in which Danielle, in using a 'that' phrase, believes correctly on general grounds (e.g., being told by someone else) that there is a unique person swimming across Lake Tahoe at the present time. Danielle has the descriptive intention to talk about the thing satisfying the property of *being a person swimming across Lake Tahoe now.* Danielle says

(2)   That person swimming across Lake Tahoe now must be cold.

In such a case, the property determined by Danielle's intention seems to be just the property of being a person swimming across Lake Tahoe at the time of utterance. But the latter is the property expressed by the predicative material occurring in the 'that' phrase. In such a case, Danielle's intention doesn't *significantly* supplement the predicative material combined with 'that' at all, since her intention and the predicative material determine/express the same property.[13] In such a case, let us say that the speaker's intentions are *redundant*.

Having seen how the properties determined by speakers' intentions figure in the semantics of 'that' phrases, we must now specify the relation that is the meaning of 'that' on the present account. On this view, 'that' ("outside of any context") expresses the following four-place relation: __ *and* __*'s unique instance in* __ *is* __, where the first, second, and final argument places are property argument places. When a speaker uses 'that' in a context (which we can think of as at least a three-tuple of an agent, time, and world), two of those argument places are filled by the property O^* determined by the speaker's intention and the world and time (w,t) of the context, yielding the following two-place relation between properties: __ *and* O^**'s unique instance in w,t is* __. This relation is then a constituent of the proposition expressed by the speaker's utterance of 'That A is B' in the context in question. Thus, assuming 'A' and 'B' express the properties A^* and B^* respectively, the speaker's utterance of 'That A is B' in this context would express the proposition that A^* stands in the relation in question to B^*. That is, the utterance expresses the proposition that A^* and O^*'s unique instance in w,t is B^*. Note that 'that' will express different relations between properties given speaker intentions that determine different properties or distinct contexts c and c' whose worlds or times are different.

When I discussed perceptual intentions, I mentioned they determine two properties, namely, the property of being the object of the perceptual intention (a relational property had by the object of the intention, consisting in bearing causal and possibly other relations to the haver of the intention), and the property of being identical to b, where b is the object of the intention. The question is, on the present theory, which of these saturates the second argument place in the four-place relation expressed by 'that' (and so plays the role of O* above) when a speaker uses a 'that' phrase with a perceptual intention? The present theory claims it is the relational property of being the object of the perceptual intention.

My main concern in defending this view in earlier work, aside from displaying data that militates against direct reference accounts and in favor of quantificational accounts, was to show that a quantificational account could handle data of the sort direct reference theorists focus on. I also claimed that this theory could handle additional data not amenable to a direct reference treatment. However, I realized there were problems, though I had not then thoroughly thought them through. Thus I repeatedly referred to the theory as a "first approximation" to the correct account. I am glad that I added this qualification, because I now believe this theory is fatally flawed. However, before getting to that, and because it is good preparation for what is to come, let us work through how the theory handles data of the sort direct reference theorists focus on.

Consider the following sentence:

(3) That man with the mohawk and pierced eyebrow is a musician

uttered in a context c (whose world and time are w,t) by a speaker S who is perceiving Ron and intends to talk about him by means of the 'that' phrase (where Ron is a man with a mohawk and pierced eyebrow). In working through this example, it will be instructive to contrast the ways in which a direct reference account and the present account capture the rigidity of the 'that' phrase in it. Thus let us begin by describing the rigidity here in a theory-neutral way, and then go on to discuss how both views capture it.

To be neutral (for the moment) on the question of whether 'that' phrases are quantificational or referring expressions, let us say that the 'that' phrase in (3) as uttered in *c determines* Ron. Consider the proposition expressed by (3) in the context as described. Call this proposition M. Most people have the intuition that whether M *would have been true* in some counterfactual circumstance depends only on whether *Ron* is a musician in that circumstance. This intuition suggests that the truth-value in a counterfactual circumstance of the proposition expressed in a context by a sentence containing a 'that' phrase such as the one in (3) above always depends on the properties in that circumstance of the individual determined by the 'that' phrase *in the original context* (and that the individual in question need not satisfy the descriptive material combined with 'that' in forming the 'that' phrase *in the circumstance in question* for the proposition to be true in that circumstance; e.g., M can be true in a circumstance in which Ron has no mohawk or piercings).

To summarize, the truth-value in a counterfactual circumstance of the proposition expressed by (3) in the context in which it was uttered depends on the properties in the counterfactual circumstance of the individual determined by the 'that' phrase *in that original context*. This is what the rigidity of 'that' phrases comes to, and this is what any theory of them must capture.

The direct reference theorist explains the rigidity of 'that' phrases elegantly. 'That' phrases contribute only the individuals they determine (by means of their characters) in the contexts in which they are used to the propositions expressed in those contexts by the sentences containing them (e.g., the proposition expressed by (3) as uttered in c has only Ron and the property of being a musician as constituents). The individuals so determined are, in Kaplan's colorful phrase, "loaded into" the proposition. Thus, when the proposition is evaluated in other circumstances, it is always the individual determined by the 'that' phrase in the context of utterance whose properties are relevant to the truth or falsity of the proposition. Further, since the 'that' phrase contributes *only* the individual so determined to the proposition, the truth of the proposition in some other circumstance does not require that the individual possess *in that circumstance* the property expressed by the descriptive material combined with 'that' in forming the 'that' phrase (e.g., M may be true in a circumstance in which Ron has no mohawk or piercings).

The present view has a quite different account of the rigidity of 'that' phrases. Recall that in uttering (3), S in w,t was perceiving and intending to talk about Ron by means of the 'that' phrase she employed. Thus, S had a perceptual intention whose object was Ron. So on the present view, the proposition expressed by (3) in the context as described is: *the unique instance of being a man with a mohawk and pierced eyebrow and O^* in w,t has the property of being a musician*, where O^* is the property determined by S's intention—in this case the property of being the object of S's current perceptual intention (of course, Ron uniquely possesses this property in w,t). Call this proposition P. Note that P's truth or falsity in counterfactual circumstances will depend on whether *Ron*, mohawked and pierced or not, is a musician in those circumstances. For when we evaluate P (*the unique instance of being a man with a mohawk and pierced eyebrow and O^* in w,t has* *the property of being a musician*) in a counterfactual situation e, we are directed to find the unique instance *in w,t* (the context of utterance) of *being a man with a mohawk and pierced eyebrow and* O^*, and see whether that thing is a musician in e. But regardless of what e is like, *Ron* is the unique instance in w,t of *being a man with a mohawk and pierced eyebrow and* O^*. And so the truth of P in e depends on whether Ron, the unique instance of being a man with a mohawk and pierced eyebrow and O^* in w,t, is a musician *in e*. Thus we have the result that when evaluating P in any circumstance e, we must always determine whether the unique instance in w,t of *being a man with a mohawk and pierced eyebrow and* O^*, that is, *Ron*, is a musician in e. In other words, P is true in an arbitrary circumstance e iff Ron is a musician in e. This is because, very roughly, on the present view a 'that' phrases make a contribution to a proposition such that when that proposition is evaluated in an arbitrary circumstance, the propositional contribution of the 'that' phrase instructs us to go back to the original context of utterance and find the individual satisfying certain conditions *in that context*. Thus the same individual is selected regardless of the circumstance in which the proposition is being evaluated. In this way, the present view captures the rigidity of 'that' phrases without holding that they are directly referential.

The view has virtues beyond capturing the rigidity of 'that' phrases. But since these have been discussed elsewhere, let me turn to what I view as the fatal flaw with the present theory.[14] It should be clear from my discussion of rigidity above that the current account of 'that' phrases makes all uses of 'that' phrases rigid. Though I believe 'that' phrases are rigid in many uses (e.g., the use of the 'that' phrase in (3) described above), some uses seem to me to be clearly nonrigid. Indeed, I have already claimed in chapter 1 that (at least some) NDNS uses are nonrigid (see example (3) of that chapter and the surrounding discussion). But it is perhaps even more clear that QI uses fail to be rigid. Thus consider the following QI use:

(4)   Every university professor cherishes that first publication of hers.

For simplicity, assume the speaker's intentions are redundant here.[15] On a quantificational account of 'that' phrases, this is simply an example of one quantifier phrase ('Every university professor') taking wide scope over and binding variables in another ('that first publication of hers'). Without going through the details, let me simply claim that on the present view (4) expresses the proposition that for every professor x, x cherishes the unique instance in w,t of being x's first publication.[16] But this seems clearly incorrect. Suppose we were to evaluate the proposition expressed by (4) in the context described, whose world and time are w,t, at another possible world w'. Suppose that every university professor at w' exists and is a university professor at w too, and that every university professor at w' published in w' what in w was her first publication. But suppose that in w', this publication failed to be her first publication. In particular suppose for each professor in w' her first publication in w was her *second* publication in w'. Finally, suppose that in w', every professor cherishes her second publication *in w'* but not her first publication *in w'*. Question: is the proposition expressed by (4) in the context described true or false in w'? It seems to me clear that it is false. But if (4) in the context described expressed the proposition that for every professor x, x cherishes the unique instance in w,t of being x's first publication, than the proposition expressed by (4) would be true in w'. For each professor in w' cherishes her first publication *in w,t* (i.e., her second publication *in w'*).

I believe that this shows that the present account of 'that' phrases is incorrect and, more specifically, that the QI use in (4) in the context as described is nonrigid.[17] As I said before, I also think some uses of 'that' phrases *are* rigid. Some might react to this situation by claiming that 'that' phrases are ambiguous, and thus that different semantic theories must be given for (at least) the rigid and nonrigid uses. Because I will directly address this concern in chapter 5, let us put it aside for now.

The next two quantificational accounts I discuss will provide a univocal semantic theory for 'that' phrases according to which some uses are rigid and some are not. Both theories attempt to provide principled explanations as to *why* some uses are rigid and others are not. Though the two theories handle rigid uses of 'that' phrases in slightly different ways, the two theories agree on which uses are rigid and which are not. Thus let us discuss this point before turning to the second of our three theories.

All the theories we shall look at agree on the following point: there are (at least) two fundamentally different kinds of intentions speakers have in using 'that' phrases. These, of course, are descriptive intentions and perceptual intentions. And it might reasonably be thought that it is which of these two kinds of intentions a speaker has in using a 'that' phrase that determines whether the use is rigid or not. After all, in having a perceptual intention, a speaker intends to "talk about" a particular object, and in having a descriptive intention, not. This might, by whatever mechanism, result in uses involving an intention of the former kind being rigid and uses involving intentions of the latter kind not being rigid (except in unusual cases). And indeed, both of the next two theories claim just this.

I think that the best way to proceed at this point is to sketch the remaining two quantificational theories and then to apply both to a certain range of data. This will have the effect of making the discussion somewhat abstract at the outset. But the hope is that the theories and their differences will be best understood by applying them side by side to the same data, rather than in succession.

The next quantificational theory I wish to discuss holds that the lexical meaning of 'that' (what it expresses "outside of any context") is a *three*-place relation. As with the previous account, when a speaker uses a 'that' phrase, the speaker's intentions determine a property that saturates the second argument place in the three-place relation expressed by 'that', thereby further restricting the quantification expressed and yielding a *two*-place relation. The resulting two-place relation is contributed by 'that' to the proposition expressed by the sentence as uttered in that context.

On the present view, 'that' expresses the relation:__ *and* __'s unique common instance is __. Here we have no argument place for the world and time of the context of utterance, as we did in the previous account. Since this was responsible for making uses of 'that' phrases rigid on the previous account (though, unfortunately, it made all uses rigid) and since we still think that *some* uses of 'that' phrase are rigid, some other mechanism must make some uses rigid on the present account. The present account holds that when a speaker has a perceptual intention whose object is b, that intention uniquely determines the property of *being identical to b* (or =b), which then saturates the second argument place in the three-place relation expressed by 'that'. And, of course, the resulting two-place relation, __ *and* =b's *unique instance is* __, is then the propositional contribution of that use of 'that'. Thus, if a speaker utters 'That F is G' with a perceptual intention whose object is b, she expresses the proposition that F^* and being identical to b's unique instance is G^*, where F^* and G^* are the properties expressed by 'F' and 'G', respectively. As is likely already apparent, the presence of the property *being identical to b* in the second argument place here makes the use of the 'that' phrase rigid. In any case this will become clear in the applications to follow.

Of course, when a speaker has a descriptive intention, the intention determines some property O^* that saturates the second argument place in the three-place relation expressed by 'that'. And, again, the resulting two-place relation, __ *and O^*'s unique instance is* __, is the propositional contribution of that use of 'that'. Thus, if a speaker utters 'That F is G' with a descriptive intention that determines the property O^*, she expresses the proposition that F^* and O^*'s unique instance is G^*, with F^* and G^* as above. In all cases of this sort except very unusual ones, this property saturating the second argument place in the three-place relation expressed by 'that' will not make the 'that' phrase rigid (as *being identical to b* did).

Thus the present theory predicts that, unusual cases aside, 'that' phrases used with perceptual intentions will be rigid and that those used with descriptive intentions will not be. This is simply a consequence of the fact that in general, the kinds of properties that are determined by the speaker's intentions and hence further restrict the quantification in these two cases are different. In the case of perceptual intentions, the property determined by the speaker's intentions (*being identical to b*) is instantiated by at most one thing in every world and the same thing in every world in which it is instantiated. Not so in usual cases for the property determined by a speaker's *descriptive* intention. Again, this will be illustrated below.

The final account of 'that' phrases we shall discuss holds that the lexical meaning of 'that' is the following *four*-place relation: __ *and* __ *are uniquely* __ *in an object x and x is* __. The first, second, and final argument places here are argument places for properties of individuals.

When a speaker uses a 'that' phrase in a context, the second argument place is saturated by a property determined by speakers' intentions of the sort discussed earlier. As on the previous theory, when a speaker has a perceptual intention whose object is b, the intention determines the property of *being identical to b*. And, again as before, when a speaker has a descriptive intention to talk about "whatever satisfies some property or conjunction of properties O^*," the intention determines O^*. As on the previous two theories, these properties, by saturating the second argument place in the four-place relation expressed by 'that', serve to restrict the quantification expressed by the 'that' phrase. The result of this saturation, of course, is a three-place relation, two of whose argument places are appropriate for properties of individuals.

The present theory holds that speakers' intentions determine another property when speakers use 'that' phrases. This property will saturate the *third* argument place in the four-place relation expressed by 'that'. Which property this is depends on the sort of intention a speaker has in using the 'that' phrase we are considering. The nature of these properties and how speakers' intentions determine them requires some discussion.

On the view under discussion, when a speaker uses a 'that' phrase with a perceptual intention whose object is b, the intention determines the property of *being identical to b*. The reason is that the speaker has formed the intention to use the 'that' phrase to talk about the object b that she is perceiving. Thus in uttering 'That F is G', the speaker is generally trying to use 'That F' to get her audience to recognize the object of her intention b, and she wants to assert that the object is G. In general, she gets her audience to recognize the object by choosing a predicate, in this case 'F', that expresses a property she believes b to possess in the context of her utterance and that she believes her audience will recognize *b* to possess in the context of her utterance. Thus, the predicates '*F*' and '*G*' have very different roles here. The speaker presumes that her audience will already recognize that the object of her intention satisfies the predicate '*F*', but she wishes to inform them that this object also satisfies '*G*'. This results in an asymmetry in the roles played by the properties expressed by '*F*' and '*G*' in the truth conditions of the proposition expressed in a context *c* by a sentence like 'That *F* is *G*.' Such a sentence, as uttered in a context *c*, expresses a proposition whose truth at an arbitrary circumstance of evaluation *e* requires b to possess in *e* the property expressed by '*G*' but does not require b to possess in *e* the property expressed by '*F*'.

On the present view, we get this consequence in the following way. We claim that when the speaker uses a 'that' phrase with a perceptual intention whose object is b in a context *c* whose world and time are w,t, her intentions determine a property of pairs (or more generally collections) of properties: the property of *being jointly instantiated in w,t*. As I have suggested, this property then saturates the third argument place in the four-place relation expressed by 'that'. Putting this together with the ideas sketched earlier about the other property determined by the speaker's intentions in such a case, namely, the property of being identical to b, we have the following view. If a speaker utters 'That *F* is *G*' with a perceptual intention whose object is b in a context whose world and time are w,t, the four-place relation expressed by 'that' has two of its argument places saturated by properties determined by the speaker's intentions. These properties are the property of *being identical to b*, which saturates the second argument place in the four-place relation expressed by 'that', and the property of *being jointly instantiated in w,t*, which saturates the third argument place in the four-place relation expressed by 'that'. The result is the following two-place

THREE QUANTIFICATIONAL ACCOUNTS OF 'THAT' PHRASES

relation between properties, which 'that' contributes to the proposition expressed: __ *and* =*b are uniquely jointly instantiated in w,t in an object x and x is* __. The sentence 'That *F* is *G*' in such a case thus expresses the proposition that F^* and =b are uniquely jointly instantiated in w,t in an object x and x is G^*, where F^* and G^* are the properties expressed by the predicates '*F*' and '*G*', respectively.

Note that among other things, this proposition predicates the property of *being jointly instantiated in w,t* of the pair of properties F^* and =b, where the property *being jointly instantiated in w,t* is determined by the intention of the speaker. Because the speaker intends to talk about b and is using the predicate '*F*' to pick out b in the context of utterance in such a case, the speaker intends to express a proposition that tracks b across worlds and times, *regardless of its possession of the property expressed by 'F' at those worlds and times*. This is why the speaker's intentions determine the property of being jointly instantiated *in w,t* in such cases. For the presence of this property in the proposition she expresses allows it to be true at worlds where b lacks the property expressed by '*F*', just as she intends. As may be obvious, such uses of 'that' phrases will be rigid, and sentences containing them will express propositions whose truth at an arbitrary world w' do not require b to possess the property expressed by '*F*' at w'.

But now consider a case in which a speaker uses a 'that' phrase but has a descriptive intention instead of a perceptual one. Thus the speaker believes that something uniquely satisfies some property or conjunction of properties and wants to make an assertion about the thing uniquely possessing those properties. As opposed to the case previously considered, in uttering 'That *F* is *G*', the speaker is not here trying to use 'That *F*' to pick out the object of his intention, and assert that it is *G*. Thus, the asymmetry in the roles played by the properties expressed by 'F' and 'G' in the proposition expressed in a context c by a sentence like 'That F is G' noted in the previous case is not present here. In particular, since the speaker has no individual in mind in such a case, he does not intend to express a proposition that tracks a particular thing across worlds and times regardless of its possession of the property expressed by 'F'. His intention seems to be to claim that something uniquely jointly instantiates the property expressed by 'F' and a property determined by his descriptive intention, and that it also possesses the property expressed by 'G'. Thus for the proposition he expresses in such a case to be true at an arbitrary circumstance of evaluation e, some unique thing must possess in e the property determined by his intentions as well the property expressed by 'F'; and that thing must of course possess in e the property expressed by 'G'.

On the present view, the mechanics of all this are as follows. When a speaker uses a 'that' phrase with a descriptive intention, so that there is no particular thing she intends to talk about, her intentions determine the property of pairs (or collections) of properties of *being jointly instantiated*. The property of *being jointly instantiated* differs importantly from the property of *being jointly instantiated at w,t*. (for particular world and time w,t). *Being jointly instantiated* is a property a pair of properties possess at some worlds, those where they have a common instance, and fail to possess at other worlds. But if a pair of properties possesses at w,t, the property of *being jointly instantiated at w,t*, then it possesses this property at every world and time.[18] Thus, in cases in which a speaker uses a 'that' phrase with a descriptive intention, her intention determines *both* a property or conjunction of properties, the unique satisfier of which she intends to talk about, *and* the property of pairs of properties of *being jointly instantiated*. The former property occupies the second argument place in the four-place relation expressed by 'that', and the latter property occupies the third argument place.

Thus, in such a case when a speaker utters 'That F is G', where her descriptive intention determines the property O^*, O^* saturates the second argument place in the four-place relation expressed by 'that' and the property of *being jointly instantiated* occupies the third argument place. As a result, 'that' contributes to the proposition expressed by the sentence the two-place relation between properties: __ *and O^* are uniquely jointly instantiated in an object x and x is* __. And the sentence as a whole expresses the proposition that F^* and O^* are uniquely jointly instantiated in an object x and x is G^*, where F^* and G^* are the properties expressed by the predicates 'F' and 'G', respectively. Note that this proposition predicates the property of *being jointly instantiated* of F^* and O^*, where, again, the property *being jointly instantiated* is determined by the intention of the speaker. As may be obvious, in usual cases of this sort the 'that' phrase will be nonrigid; and sentences containing uses of 'that' phrases of this sort will express propositions whose truth at an arbitrary world w' require something to possess the property expressed by 'F' at w'.

Now that we have sketched our final two theories of 'that' phrases, let us apply them to some examples to illustrate the theories and their differences. In particular, we shall consider an NDNS use, a QI use, and a "classic demonstrative" use. For ease of reference, let us call the first of the theories sketched T_1 and the second T_2.

So let us consider an NDNS use of a 'that' phrase. I claim that in typical NDNS uses, speaker intentions are redundant. The reason for this is that since the speaker does not have a particular individual in mind and so is not making use of a demonstration, in the general case the audience will have no way of knowing the speaker's intentions and the property they determine. Thus the speaker combines 'that' with predicative material that expresses the property that his intentions determine because this is often the only way to provide the audience access to the property determined by his intentions. The result is that his intentions are redundant. Consider again Scott lecturing his class on hominid discoveries. As before, he says:

(5)   That hominid who discovered how to start fires was a genius.

Again, Scott's use of the 'that' phrase here is clearly an NDNS use. He employs no demonstration, obviously has no particular individual "in mind" as the individual he intends to talk about, and clearly is not talking about any creature in the physical context of his utterance. In this case, Scott intends to talk about "the thing possessing the property of *being a hominid who discovered how to start fires*." Thus he has a descriptive intention that determines the property of *being a hominid who discovered how to start fires*. So Scott's intention is redundant (his intention determining the same property expressed by the predicative material combined with 'that'). I hasten to add that there are NDNS uses in which speaker intentions are not redundant, and we will consider such cases later. But for the purposes of comparing T1 and T2 such additional complexity is irrelevant.

T1 claims that in such a case, the property determined by the speaker's intention, *being a hominid who discovered how to start fires*, saturates the second argument place of the three-place relation expressed by 'that'. Thus, 'that' contributes to the proposition expressed by (5) in such a case the two-place relation between properties __ *and being a hominid who discovered how to start fires' unique common instance is* __. And the sentence expresses the proposition that *being a hominid who discovered how to start fires* and *being a hominid who discovered how to start fires*' unique common instance was a genius (note the redundancy). The truth of this proposition in an arbitrary circumstance of evaluation e requires being a hominid who discovered how to start fires to have a unique instance x in e and x must be a genius in e. So the truth of the proposition does not require the *same* individual to possess any of these properties in e as possesses them in the original context of utterance. That is, the 'that' phrase is not rigid.

T2 holds that the property determined by the speaker's intention, *being a hominid who discovered how to start fires*, saturates the second argument place of the *four*-place relation expressed by 'that'. Further, since Scott has a descriptive intention, his intention determines the property of pairs of properties of *being jointly instantiated*, which then saturates the *third* argument place in the four-place relation expressed by 'that'. Thus, on T2 Scott's utterance of (5) in the situation as described expresses a proposition to the effect that being a hominid who discovered how to start fires and being a hominid who discovered how to start fires are uniquely jointly instantiated in an object x, and x was a genius (note the redundancy). The truth of this proposition in an arbitrary circumstance of evaluation e requires being a hominid who discovered how to start fires to have a unique instance x in e, and x must be a genius in e. So the truth of the proposition does not require the *same* individual to possess any of these properties in e as possesses them in the original context of utterance. That is, the 'that' phrase is not rigid.

So T1 and T2 both claim that the 'that' phrase in (5) as used in the situation as described is nonrigid (as we claimed in chapter 1); and the propositions they claim are expressed in such a case have the same truth conditions and thus are necessarily equivalent.[19] Clearly, there isn't much to choose between these two theories in such cases.

Before considering how T1 and T2 handle QI uses, it is worth briefly discussing sentences containing a 'that' phrase and another quantifier phrase, where the other quantifier does *not* bind a pronoun/variable in the 'that' phrase. So consider a sentence such as:

(6)   Every skier loves that mountain.

Let us suppose that (6) is uttered by a speaker in w, t who is perceiving, intending to talk about, and demonstrating the mountain KT-22. Since on T1 and T2 there are two quantifiers in (6), both will hold that it has a scope ambiguity and so expresses two different propositions. According to T1, (6) in the context in question expresses the following propositions:

(6a)   [[Every skier: x] [[THAT$_{=k}$ mountain: y]
[x loves y]]]

(6b)   [[THAT$_{=k}$ mountain: y] [[Every skier: x]
[x loves y]]]

(where THAT$_{=k}$ is the three-place relation T1 claims 'that' expresses with its second argument place filled by the property of being identical to KT-22). (6a) is true iff for every skier x, being a mountain and being identical to KT-22 have a unique common instance y and x loves y. (6b) is true iff being a mountain and being identical to KT-22 have a unique common instance y and for every skier x, x loves y. Thus, (6a) and (6b) have the same truth conditions. The difference in the relative scopes of the quantifiers makes no truth-conditional difference.

Similarly, on T2 (6) in the context described expresses the following two propositions:

(6c)   [[Every skier: x] [[THAT$_{=k, Jwt}$ mountain: y]
[x loves y]]]

(6d)   [[THAT$_{=k, \text{J}wt}$ mountain: y] [[Every skier: x]
[x loves y]]]

(where THAT$_{=k, \text{J}wt}$ is the four-place relation T2 claims
'that' expresses with its second and third argument places
saturated by being identical to KT-22 and being jointly
instantiated in w,t, respectively). (6c) is true iff for every
skier x, being identical to KT-22 and being a mountain are
uniquely jointly instantiated in w,t in an object y and x
loves y. (6d) is true iff being identical to KT-22 and being
a mountain are uniquely jointly instantiated in w,t in an
object y and for every skier x, x loves y. So here again, the
scope ambiguity makes no truth-conditional difference.
Thus, both T1 and T2 claim, correctly, that a sentence like
(6) (taken as uttered in a context) has only one set of truth
conditions.[20] Though we imagined that the 'that' phrase in
(6) had a "classic demonstrative" use, the same would be
true if the 'that' phrase had an NDNS use instead.

Let us now turn to a QI use and see how our two
theories handle it. Before doing that, however, we must
digress briefly and address a complication that we have
thus far suppressed. Thus far I have said that in using 'that'
phrases, speaker intentions determine *properties*, which
then saturate the second argument place of the three- or
four-place relation expressed by the determiner 'that'
(depending on which of our two theories is being considered), thereby restricting the quantification it expresses.
Further, I have suggested that the predicative material
combined with the determiner 'that' in forming a 'that'
phrase contributes a *property* to the proposition expressed
by the sentence containing the 'that' phrase. However,
neither of these claims is true in the general case. Beginning
with the latter point, let us consider the propositions
expressed by sentences in which one quantifier phrase
binds variables (pronouns) in another quantifier phrase,
such as

(7) Every man loves some woman he kissed.

The reading of (7) on which 'he' is a variable bound by the quantifier 'Every man' results from (7) expressing something like the following proposition:

(7a) [[Every* x [man*x]] [some* y [woman* y & x kissed* y]] [x loves* y]]

where e^* is the propositional contribution of the expression e (e.g., kissed*, the kissing relation, is the contribution of 'kissed'; every* is the relation between properties expressed by 'every', etc.). What is the propositional contribution of the predicative material 'woman he kissed', which is combined with 'some' to form the quantifier 'some woman he kissed'? It is the *two-place relation* [woman*y and x kissed* y].[21] Thus in cases in which one quantifier phrase binds variables in another quantifier phrase, the predicative material combining with the determiner to form the latter quantifier phrase contributes a *relation* to a proposition. On the present account this is exactly what happens in examples like:

(8) Most avid snow skiers remember that first black diamond run they attempted to ski.

Again we have one quantifier phrase ('Most avid snow skiers') taking wide scope over and binding variables in another ('that first black diamond they attempted to ski').

In a typical case of an utterance of (8), what intention will the speaker have in using the 'that' phrase? Intuitively, the speaker intends to use the phrase to talk about first black diamond runs attempted by most avid skiers. That is, the speaker intends to talk about the unique instance of *being x's first black diamond run attempted* for most avid skiers x. Thus the speaker's intentions determine the relation *being x's first black diamond run attempted*. Call this relation Ryx (y is x's first black diamond run attempted).

THREE QUANTIFICATIONAL ACCOUNTS OF 'THAT' PHRASES

The speaker's intention determines more than just this relation. The intention must also distinguish between the x and y argument places in R. After all, in using the 'that' phrase the speaker intended to make a claim about the unique instance y of Ryx for most avid skiers x. Thus the speaker's intention determines the relation Ryx, and, as a result of the speaker intending to talk about the unique y such that Ryx for most avid skiers x, distinguishes between the x and y argument places.

Since the speaker's intention determines the relation Ryx, this relation saturates the second argument place in the three- or four-place relation expressed by 'that' that in earlier cases was saturated by a *property* determined by speaker intentions. However, since this relation is also expressed by the predicative material combined with 'that' in forming the quantifier 'that first publication of his', the speaker's intention is redundant in such a case.

As with NDNS uses, such cases are typical for QI uses. A speaker will typically have a descriptive intention in using the 'that' phrase (e.g., in uttering (8), a speaker will typically have the intention to talk about the unique instance of being x's first black diamond run attempted for most avid skiers x) and since she will have no way of giving her audience access to her intention, she will combine 'that' with predicative material that expresses the same relation determined by her intentions. Thus her intentions will be redundant. And, as with NDNS uses, I hasten to add that there are QI uses in which intentions are not redundant. We shall consider such uses later. But here, as in NDNS cases, the additional complexity involved in such uses is irrelevant to comparing T1 and T2.

With these preliminaries behind us, let us look at how T1 and T2 treat (8), which I repeat here for convenience:

(8) Most avid snow skiers remember that first black diamond run they attempted to ski.

Assuming as we are that intentions are redundant, on T1 (8) expresses the proposition that for most avid snow skiers x, the unique instance y of being the first black diamond run x attempted is such that x remembers y. Here the predicative material combined with 'that' in the 'that' phrase ('first black diamond run they attempted to ski') contributes a relation to the proposition expressed by (8) (y is the first black diamond run x attempted to ski) just as happened with (7) above.[22]

Note that the proposition expressed by (8) in the situation described according to T1 is true at an arbitrary circumstance of evaluation e iff for most avid skiers x in e, the unique instance y of being the first black diamond run x attempted to ski in e is such that x remembers y in e. Thus, the 'that' phrase in (8) is nonrigid: when the proposition expressed by (8) in the context as described is evaluated in an arbitrary circumstance e, the "quantificational contribution" of the 'that' phrase "picks out" for different avid skiers in e, the unique black diamond run they first attempted to ski in e, not in the world of the context of utterance of (8). Intuitively, this certainly seems the correct result, as I noted in discussing why I no longer favor the view I defended in previous work.

Let us consider how T2 handles (8) in the situation as described. Obviously, in uttering (8), the speaker does not have a perceptual intention, since she is not intending to talk about any particular ski run. Thus, she has a descriptive intention. This in turn means that her intention determines the property of pairs of properties of *being jointly instantiated*, which saturates the third argument place in the four-place relation expressed by 'that'. Recall that we are also assuming that her intentions are redundant, determining the same relation that is expressed by the descriptive material in the 'that' phrase. Still, though it does so to no semantically significant effect, this relation saturates the second argument place in the four-place relation expressed by 'that'. Thus, in uttering (8) the speaker expresses a proposition to the effect that most avid snow skiers x remember a y such that y uniquely instantiates being the first black diamond run x attempted to ski.[23] Note that this proposition is true at an arbitrary circumstance of evaluation e iff roughly, in e, most avid skiers in e remember the unique instance of being a first black diamond run they attempted to ski *in e*. Thus, as on T1, the 'that' phrase in (8) is nonrigid: when the proposition expressed by (8) in the context as described is evaluated in an arbitrary circumstance e, the "quantificational contribution" of the 'that' phrase "picks out," for different avid skiers in e, the unique black diamond run they first attempted to ski *in e*, not in the world of the context of utterance of (8).

Here again, as in NDNS cases, T1 and T2 both appear to get the correct results and yield necessarily equivalent propositions. And so here again, there are no grounds for choosing between the theories. However, as we shall see, T1 and T2 make importantly different predictions about "classic demonstrative" uses of 'that' phrases. To such uses we now turn.

Consider a particular use of a 'that' phrase with a perceptual intention. Suppose that Caitlin is looking at Colin driving his red Blazer, forms the intention to say something about him, and decides to use a 'that' phrase to do so. Pointing at Colin, she says

(9)   That guy driving the red Blazer is smart.

T1 and T2 agree that Caitlin's intention determines the property of being identical to Colin.

T1 claims that this property saturates the second argument place in the three-place relation expressed by 'that'. Thus, (9) expresses the proposition that being a guy driving the red Blazer and being identical to Colin have a unique common instance and it is smart. If we evaluate this proposition at an arbitrary circumstance of evaluation e, we are to see whether being identical to Colin and being a guy driving a red Blazer have a unique instance in e, which is also smart in e. Since Colin is the only thing that possesses the property of being identical to Colin in any possible world, only Colin can be the unique instance of being identical to Colin and being a guy driving a red Blazer in e. So for there to be a unique instance of being identical to Colin and being a guy driving a red Blazer in e it is necessary and sufficient that Colin be a guy driving a red Blazer in e. Thus, (9) is true at an arbitrary circumstance of evaluation e iff Colin is a guy driving a red Blazer there and is smart there. Thus, the use of the 'that' phrase in (9) is rigid: the truth of the proposition it expresses at an arbitrary circumstance always depends on Colin's properties in that circumstance.

According to T2, Caitlin's intention determines the property of individuals of *being identical to Colin* and the property of pairs of properties of *being jointly instantiated in w,t*, where w and t are the world and time of the context of Caitlin's utterance. Thus Caitlin's utterance of (9) expresses a proposition to the effect that being a guy driving a red Blazer and being identical to Colin are uniquely jointly instantiated in w,t in an object x and x is smart. Thus on T2, the proposition expressed by (9) in the context as described is true in an arbitrary circumstance of evaluation e iff there is a unique common instance of being identical to Colin and being a guy driving a red Blazer *in w,t* (the world and time of the context of utterance), and the thing in question is smart *in e*. Thus, so long as Colin is driving a red Blazer in the context of utterance, the proposition expressed by (9) is true in an arbitrary circumstance of evaluation e iff Colin is smart in e. Therefore, the truth in an arbitrary circumstance e of the proposition expressed by (9) in the context as described always depends on *Colin's* properties in e and doesn't require Colin to be driving a red Blazer in e.

Hence the 'that' phrase in (9) when uttered in the situation as described is rigid on both T_1 and T_2. However, the propositions T_1 and T_2 claim are expressed by (9) in such a case have different truth conditions. T_1 claims that for the proposition expressed to be true at an arbitrary circumstance of evaluation e, Colin must be a guy driving a red Blazer *in e* as well as smart in e. T_2 claims that for the proposition expressed to be true at e, Colin must be a guy driving a red Blazer *in w,t* (the world and time of Caitlin's context of utterance) and must be smart *in e*.

It seems to me that T_2 is correct here. Most people have the intuition that the truth of the proposition expressed by (9) in the situation described in an arbitrary circumstance of evaluation e requires only that Colin be smart in e. This intuition is strengthened if we consider an example in which the predicative material in the 'that' phrase expresses a *very* ephemeral property (even more ephemeral than driving a Red Blazer!) of the thing that the speaker intends to talk about by means of the 'that' phrase. For example, suppose I see someone, say, Alan, crossing the street, and, intending to talk about him, I point at him and say:

(10) That guy crossing the street is an idiot.

Many have a strong intuition that whether the proposition I expressed (what-I-said, as the Kaplanians say) would have been true in this or that circumstance of evaluation depends only on whether Alan is an idiot in that circumstance. He is not in addition required to be crossing the street in the circumstance in question. I admit to having this intuition myself. Such intuitions support T_2 over T_1.

A second consideration militates against T1's claim that an utterance of 'That F is G', when 'That F' has a classic demonstrative use, expresses a proposition whose truth at an arbitrary circumstance of evaluation requires the thing the speaker intended to talk about to be F at that circumstance. Consider the following sentence:

(11)   It is possible that that senator from California is a crook

(i.e., it is possible that that senator from California should have been a crook).[24] Imagine that I utter (11) as I point at a man, b, sitting in the corner of a bar. My perceptual intention determines the property of *being identical to b* in such a case and T1 claims that this property saturates the second argument place in the three-place relation expressed by 'that'. Of course, (11) should exhibit a scope ambiguity. The two readings T1 assigns (11) may be represented as follows:

(11a)   [THAT$_{=b}$ senator from California: x] [Possibly [x is a crook]]

(11b)   Possibly [[THAT$_{=b}$ senator from California: x] [x is a crook]]

(where THAT$_{=b}$ is the three-place relation T1 claims is expressed by 'that' with the second argument place saturated by the property of being identical to b). These may be represented more colloquially as follows:

(11a′)   [being a senator from California and being identical to b have a unique common instance x] [Possibly [x is a crook]]

(11b′)   Possibly [[being a senator from California and being identical to b have a unique common instance x] [x is a crook]]

I don't doubt that (11) has a reading corresponding to
(11a)/(11a′). But it seems to me clear that (11) has no
reading corresponding to (11b)/(11b′). On this alleged
reading, (11) would be true iff it is possible that b be a
senator from California and a crook. Surely it has no such
reading. If I point at b, who is not a senator, but might
have been a senator from California and a crook and utter
(11), I have not spoken truly. So T1 predicts that (11) and
sentences like it have readings that they do not appear to
have.

T2, it should be noted, predicts that (11) has the following two readings in the situation as described:

(11c) [THAT$_{=b, Jwt}$ senator from California: x] [Possibly
[x is a crook]]

(11d) Possibly [[THAT$_{=b, Jwt}$ senator from California: x]
[x is a crook]]

where w,t are the world and time of the context of utterance and THAT$_{=b, Jwt}$ is the two-place relation resulting
from saturating the second and third argument places of
the four-place relation expressed by 'that' with the properties of *being identical to b* and *being jointly instantiated
in w,t*, respectively. Now if we confine our attention to
worlds in which b exists, (11c) and (11d) will not diverge
in truth value. (11c) is true at an arbitrary world w' iff
something x is a unique instance of being identical to b and
being a senator from California in w,t and for some world
w'' possible relative to w', x is a crook at w''. (11d) is true
at w' iff for some w'' possible relative to w', something x is
the unique instance of being identical to b and being a
senator from California in w,t and x is a crook in w''.
Intuitively, (11c) instructs us to first find the unique instance
of being identical to b and being a senator from California
in w,t, and then check whether it is a crook in w''; whereas
(11d) instructs us to first go to w'', then go back to w,t and

find the unique instance of being identical to b and being a senator from California, and then make sure that this thing is a crook in w''. Thus, it should be clear that, given our assumptions, (11c) and (11d) cannot diverge in truth value at any world.

So even though T2 claims there is a scope ambiguity in (11), subject to the assumptions we have made, the ambiguity is truth-conditionally inert. Thus it appears that T1 assigns (11) a reading it does not have, whereas T2 does not.

The advocate of T1 might attempt to respond to this point by telling some story as to how *pragmatic* considerations filter out the reading (11b). So one might hold that though the *semantics* allows the reading, pragmatic considerations ensure that it doesn't arise. I am skeptical about any such story. For it seems that sentences like (11) uttered in situations of the sort described *never* have readings corresponding to (11b). And this suggests to me that it isn't *pragmatic* considerations that filter out the reading, but that the sentence is assigned no such reading by the *semantics*. For if the explanation for the lack of the reading really is pragmatic, one would think that we should be able to come up with some situation in which the pragmatic constraints blocking the reading are relaxed, being satisfied elsewhere, allowing the reading to come through.

Let me illustrate with a pragmatic mechanism someone might want to invoke to explain the absence of the reading (11b). On T1 (as well as T2), when 'That F is G' is uttered in a situation like that described in discussing (11), for the proposition expressed to be true in the context of utterance of the sentence the demonstrated object must be F. So, one might continue, speakers use the nominal 'F' to "pragmatically help" the auditor determine what the speaker is talking about. But the fact that the nominal 'F' in 'That F is G' generally has this pragmatic function will tend to filter out the reading (11b) of (11). For (11b) can be true even when the demonstrated object is not *F* (not a senator from California), but only possibly *F*. In such a case, of course, the nominal would not be able to fulfill its pragmatic function of helping the auditor determine what the speaker is talking about.

But even if the nominal pragmatically has the function of helping the auditor determine whom the speaker is talking about, why can't the reading (11b) come through when it is independently clear to everyone whom the speaker is talking about and it is quite apparent to all that he or she is not *F*? Here pragmatic considerations should *favor* (11b). The auditor should reason (implicitly) as follows: "It is completely clear to everyone whom the speaker is talking about, and it is completely clear that that thing is not *F* (a senator from California). Thus the speaker can only intend the narrow scope reading of 'that *F*' (resulting in (11b))." To summarize, then, I cannot see how T1 is able to explain why sentences like (11) *always* lack the readings corresponding to (11b).

And indeed, I think we can see that the strategy of trying to explain away this always-missing reading (11b) of (11) cannot get around the root of the problem. For what if, in exactly the same circumstances, instead of (11) I utter:

(11′) That senator from California is a crook. That might have been true.

Here the second sentence expresses the claim that the proposition expressed by the first sentence is possible. On (T1), the proposition in question is:

(11′a) [[THAT$_{=b}$ senator from California: x] [x is a crook]]

So again, (T1) predicts that if the man I pointed at, b, is not a senator from California but might have been both a sen-

ator from California and a crook, the second sentence of
(11′) is true. But surely this is wrong! (I recommend considering additional examples to convince yourself of this.)
And here, since scope cannot be at issue, the (T1) theorist
cannot attempt to get around the argument by telling some
story about why 'that' phrases won't take narrow scope.[25]

Though I won't argue the case here, it seems that
similar problems arise with respect to other scoped elements such as tense operators, and so on.

Thus intuitions about the truth conditions of the
proposition expressed by (10) in the described situation
and the readings had (and not had) by (11) and (11′) in the
described situation suggest that T1 is incorrect and that we
ought to adopt T2.

However, Mark Richard (1993) has adduced some
considerations that might initially appear to support T1
and not T2. Thus, before turning away from T1, let us
look at these considerations.

Richard notes that sentences like the following seem
true, when the 'that' phrase is used in w,t with a perceptual
intention whose object is some dog b:[26]

(12)   Necessarily, if that dog next to Tom is asleep, then
something is next to Tom.

T1, of course, would explain this. On T1, when the 'that'
phrase is used as described, the antecedent of the embedded
conditional expresses a proposition that is true in a circumstance of evaluation e iff in e something x is the unique
instance of being identical to b and being a dog next to
Tom and in e x is asleep. But then if this proposition is true
in an arbitrary circumstance of evaluation e, b is a dog
next to Tom in e. Thus the proposition expressed by the
consequent of the embedded conditional in (12) would be
true at e. But then since in any circumstance e in which the
proposition expressed by the antecedent is true, the prop-

osition expressed by the consequent is true, (12) as a whole must be true. Thus T1 explains why (12) seems true. On T1, it is true.

By contrast, on T2 (12) is false. When the 'that' phrase is used as described, T2 predicts that the antecedent of the embedded conditional in (12) expresses the proposition that the unique instance of being identical to b and being a dog next to Tom in w,t is asleep. For this proposition to be true in an arbitrary circumstance of evaluation e, something x must be the unique instance of being identical to b and being a dog next to Tom *in w,t* (the world and time of the context of utterance of (12)) and x must be asleep in e. Thus even if this proposition is true at e, the proposition expressed by the consequent of the embedded conditional in (12) need not be. For the fact that there is a unique instance of being identical to b and being a dog next to Tom *in w,t* does not guarantee that there is something next to Tom *in e*. Thus, (12) is not true on T2, and it appears that T1 has an advantage here.

However, T2 can explain why (12) may *seem* true. Call the embedded conditional in (12) D. In any context c in which D is uttered with a perceptual intention, if the proposition expressed by the antecedent is true in c, the proposition expressed by the consequent is true in c. For let D be uttered in a context c whose world and time are w,t by a speaker whose perceptual intention has as its object b. Then the antecedent of D expresses the proposition that the unique instance of being identical to b and being a dog next to Tom in w,t is asleep. But if this is true in w,t, then something (i.e., b) is next to Tom in w,t. Thus the proposition expressed by the consequent of D is true in w,t. Thus when D is uttered in a context c whose world and time are w,t by a speaker with a perceptual intention, if the proposition expressed by the antecedent is true in w,t, so is the proposition expressed by the consequent. It is easy to see how this could create the illusion that D cannot be false and so must be necessary. Hence the apparent truth of (12), according to T2.

So both T1 and T2 have some explanation as to why (12) seems true. Perhaps T1 has a slight advantage here, because its explanation is the most straightforward: (12) *is* true. But the matter doesn't end there. There are sentences like (12) that don't seem true. For example, Richard reports that David Braun pointed out that the following sentence doesn't seem true:

(13) Necessarily, if that dog with a blue collar exists, then it has a blue collar.

Richard suggests that it is something about 'exists' (he knows not what) that makes (13) seem false. But this doesn't seem to me correct. The following example also sounds quite false to my ear:

(14) Necessarily, if that guy in the windbreaker is human, then he is wearing a windbreaker.

Of course T2 can explain why (13) and (14) seem false. They *are* false. T1, by contrast, has no obvious explanation as to why (13) and (14) seem false. Though this might seem to favor T2, it really doesn't, at least not clearly. For though T2 explains why (12) seems true and explains why (13) and (14) seem false, when you put the explanations together, something seems lacking. For T2 claims that when D (the embedded conditional in (12)) is uttered in a context c whose world and time are w,t by a speaker with a perceptual intention, then if the proposition expressed by the antecedent is true in w,t, so is the proposition expressed by the consequent. This in turn produces the illusion that (12) is true. But the same could be said of (13) and (14), so why doesn't the illusion of truth arise here?[27] Until T2 can give a principled account of why the illusion in question arises in the case of (12) and not in the case of (13) and (14), it cannot claim to have an account of the data comprising (12)–(14).

But, as already indicated, T1 has no obvious explanation of why (13) and (14) seem false. Thus until T1 has such an explanation, and one that also explains why (12) *doesn't* seem false, it cannot claim to have an adequate account of (12)–(14) either. Thus, with respect to this data, the two theories are at a stand-off. Therefore, on the basis of the previously noted advantages of T2 over T1, I hereby adopt T2.[28]

To this point we have seen how the present view (i.e., T2) handles "classic demonstrative" uses of 'that' phrases, and QI and NDNS uses with redundant intentions. However, as I mentioned in discussing these uses, there are QI and NDNS uses in which a speaker's intentions are *not* redundant. Thus before turning to other matters, we ought to take a look at such cases and how our theory treats them.

First, let us look at NDNS uses with nonredundant speakers' intentions. Before doing that, however, let me remind the reader why speaker intentions are redundant in typical NDNS uses. In such cases, the speaker does not have a particular individual in mind and so is not making use of a demonstration. Hence in the general case the audience will have no way of knowing the speaker's intentions and the property they determine. Thus the speaker combines 'that' with predicative material that expresses the property that her intentions determine because this is often the only way to provide the audience access to the property determined by her intentions. The result is that her intentions are redundant.

In attempting to sketch an NDNS use where speakers' intentions are *not* redundant, the question arises as to how we *know* that intentions really are nonredundant in the cases we discuss. Earlier, when I endorsed the claim, which is also endorsed by the direct reference theorist, that intentions are semantically relevant to 'that' phrases, I noted that this view explained certain differences between 'that' phrases and definite descriptions. In particular, if we assume that intentions are relevant to the semantics of 'that' phrases but not definite descriptions, this explains why the phrase 'that F' can be used several times in a situation in which there are many Fs to talk about distinct Fs, whereas 'the F' often cannot be. Thus, I noted that looking at cars in a lot filled with new cars, one can say 'That car is nicer than that car', talking about distinct cars by means of the distinct occurrences of 'that car', but one could not felicitously use 'the' phrases instead. 'The car is nicer than the car' (with or without accompanying demonstrations) is infelicitous. If demonstrations or speaker intentions are relevant to the semantics of 'that' phrases, different demonstrations or intentions associated with the distinct occurrences of 'that F' would allow them to be used to talk about distinct Fs, which would explain the felicity of 'That car is nicer than that car'. By contrast, the semantics of 'the' does not allow a role for demonstrations or speaker intentions. Thus, there is nothing that allows the distinct occurrences of 'the F' to be used to talk about different Fs, and so the attempt to use distinct occurrences of 'the F' to talk about distinct Fs results in infelicity (in this case at any rate).

Similarly, if Diane is on a ski lift looking down at a ski run filled with male skiers and she points at a skier and says 'I wish I could ski like that man', there is nothing odd about her remark. But if she had said instead 'I wish I could ski like the man', there certainly would be something odd about her remark.[29] Presumably the oddness is a result of the description being radically incomplete in an environment in which many things satisfy it. Again, if speaker intentions are relevant to the semantics of 'that' phrases, serving to further restrict the quantification they express, and not relevant to definite descriptions, these facts would be explained.

Thus, if we could find NDNS uses in which uses of 'that' phrases are felicitous but in which uses of exactly similar definite descriptions would be odd or infelicitous, this would provide evidence that speakers' intentions are semantically relevant here too *and* are not redundant in such cases. For if the intentions were not semantically relevant or were relevant but redundant, it is hard to see why the 'that' phrase would be felicitous and the definite description would be odd or infelicitous. In such a case the descriptive material in both the 'that' phrase and the definite description would alone provide the sole restriction on the quantification expressed. Thus both expressions would have the same semantic restriction, and so one would expect both expressions to be felicitous or not as a pair. In short, if the fact that certain "classic demonstrative" uses of 'that' phrases are felicitous where exactly similar definite descriptions are infelicitous is, as I have claimed, evidence for the claim that speakers' intentions are semantically relevant to these uses of 'that' phrases (and not redundant) and not semantically relevant to the corresponding uses of definite descriptions, then exactly similar differences between the behavior of NDNS (and QI) uses of 'that' phrases and the behavior of definite descriptions provide evidence that speakers intentions are semantically relevant to these uses *and are not redundant.*

It turns out we do find cases in which NDNS uses of 'that' phrases are felicitous and uses of exactly similar definite descriptions are not. Thus, suppose that we have together and silently (to eliminate the possibility of anaphoric connection) performed calculations that show that there is exactly one location (we don't know where) on the earth where its gravitational field is weak, allowing people to jump incredibly high in the air. Seeing the implications of our calculations, I say:

(15)   Even I could slam dunk at that place.

In this case it would seem that my intentions determine the property of *being a place where the earth's gravitational field is weak*. Because of our shared experience of performing the relevant calculations together, my audience is in a position to grasp my intention and the property it determines.[30] I express a proposition to the effect that being a place and being a place where the earth's gravitational field is weak are uniquely jointly instantiated in an object x and even I could slam dunk at x.

Most important for present purposes, note that substituting an exactly similar definite description for the 'that' phrase in (15) results in infelicity or oddness:

*(15a)   Even I could slam dunk at the place.

Presumably the oddness here results from the description being radically incomplete. And since the semantics of descriptions doesn't allow supplementation by properties determined by speaker intentions, the use of the description is infelicitous. However, the semantics of 'that' phrases does allow for such supplementation. This occurs in (15), and so the use of the 'that' phrase is felicitous. Thus here we have evidence that speakers' intentions are not redundant in some NDNS uses.

Another example concerns a case in which a group of astronomers are making calculations concerning what was visible in the night sky from Carnelian Bay at various times in the past. They are able to determine that in the year 100 A.D. the earth passed through an asteroid belt and that for exactly one night there was an incredible display of shooting stars visible from the shore at Carnelian Bay. Owing to the incompleteness of their data, they cannot determine precisely which night it was. Once they see the implications of their calculations, one astronomer says to the others:

(16)   I would give anything to have been at Carnelian Bay on that night.

Assuming his intentions determine the property of being a night in 100 A.D. when an incredible display of shooting stars was visible from the shores of Carnelian Bay, the astronomer's utterance of (16) expresses (roughly) the proposition that being a night in 100 A.D. when an incredible display of shooting stars was visible from the shores of Carnelian Bay is uniquely instantiated in an object x and the astronomer in question would give anything to have been at Carnelian Bay on x.

But the important point for present purposes is that if the astronomer who uttered (16) had instead uttered the following sentence, the result would have been infelicitous:

*(16a)   I would give anything to have been at Carnelian Bay on the night.

As before, I claim that the difference between (16) and (16a) results from the fact that the semantics of 'that' phrases allows for supplementation by properties determined by speakers' intentions whereas the semantics of 'the' does not. And so I claim that (16) and (16a) provide evidence that speakers' intentions are sometimes not redundant in NDNS uses.

A final example involves a group of senators who are at a bar. They know that exactly one senator (they don't know who) is testifying before the Senate Ethics Committee regarding campaign finance irregularities. Depending on the testimony, an investigation will be launched or not. They hear that the committee has decided to launch an investigation. One senator says to another:

(17)   I'm going to kill that senator.

Assuming his intention was to talk about the thing satisfying the property of being a senator who testified before the
Senate Ethics Committee, his utterance of (17) expresses
the proposition that being a senator who testified before
the Senate Ethics Committee is uniquely instantiated in an
object x and he (the speaker) is going to kill x. Again, for
present purposes the important point is that if the senator
instead utters the following sentence to the other senators,
the result is at least odd and possibly infelicitous:

*(17a)   I'm going to kill the senator.

Again, I claim that (17) and (17a) provide evidence that
speakers' intentions are sometimes not redundant in NDNS
uses.

Turning now to a more complex example, suppose that
Scott the scientist is strolling through the Great Moments
in Hominid History Fair he sponsors every year. Students
produce and display projects on great moments in hominid
history. On Scott's left is a project concerning the hominid
who invented the wheel. On Scott's right is a project concerning the hominid who discovered how to start fires.
Scott, tremendously admiring the latter discovery and feeling that the wheel is overrated, says:

(18)   That hominid [nodding to his right] was a lot
smarter than that hominid [nodding to his left].

Presumably, Scott, in uttering the first 'that' phrase had the
intention to "talk about" the unique instance of *being a
hominid who discovered how to start fires*; and he had the
intention to talk about the unique instance of *being a
hominid who invented the wheel* in uttering the second
'that' phrase. Thus on the present view, Scott in uttering
(18) expressed a proposition that is true iff being a hominid
who discovered how to start fires has a unique instance x

and being a hominid who invented the wheel has a unique instance y and x was a lot smarter than y. Note that when we substitute exactly similar definite descriptions for the 'that' phrases in (18) we get infelicity:

*(18a)   The hominid [nodding to his right] was a lot smarter than the hominid [nodding to his left].

So here we have evidence that the speaker's intentions are nonredundant and semantically relevant in uttering (18).

The attentive reader will understandably complain that the use in (18) is not an NDNS use at all. After all, Scott employed demonstrations. True, but I think it is an NDNS use nonetheless. First, note that the other conditions for NDNS uses are satisfied: Scott had no particular individual in mind, and the individual he intended to "talk about" certainly need not have been present in the physical context of utterance. Second, Scott and I are to be excused: we had no choice! If I use the 'that' phrases in a sentence like (18) in an NDNS way, to have any chance of speaking truly, I must associate intentions with the two 'that' phrases that determine *different* properties (otherwise, I will have said "of exactly one hominid" that he was a lot smarter than himself—something that could not be true). Further, I must make manifest to my audience these intentions and the *different* properties they determine, if I wish them to understand me. And to do this, it would seem that I must exploit current features of our shared environment, or shared memories, or some such thing and call my audience's attention to these shared features of our environment, or shared memories, etc. But in calling my audience's attention to such things, I must clearly *distinguish* the two intentions and the properties they determine for my audience, and make clear to my audience *which* of the two intentions and the properties it determines is associated with which occurrence of the 'that' phrase. *And how could*

I do this without demonstrations, nods of my head, directed glances, fortuitous occurrences, or something to that effect?

The important point is that in such cases, what is being demonstrated is *not* the thing I intend to "talk about" by means of the 'that' phrase. Again, the demonstration serves to give the audience access to some property determined by the speaker's descriptive intention. So though a demonstration is involved, it functions very differently from the way demonstrations function in "classic demonstrative" uses. Because something like a demonstration is unavoidable in such cases even when the speaker is attempting an NDNS use, because the demonstration functions so differently from the way it does in "classic demonstrative" uses, and because the other conditions on NDNS uses are present in such cases, I consider the uses in (18) in the situation described NDNS uses. In light of this, perhaps we should say that NDNS uses are those in which the 'that' phrase need not be used to talk about something present in the physical context of utterance, and in which the speaker has no particular individual in mind as "the thing she intends to talk about by means of the 'that' phrase"; and in which *if* she employs a demonstration at all, it is not used to demonstrate the object she intends to talk about but rather functions to provide the audience access to some property determined by her intentions.

I have claimed that the need for demonstrations in this case is traceable to the fact that the speaker employed two occurrences of the same 'that' phrase to talk about two different things ('that hominid' in (18)); that to do this she must have intentions that determine different properties; that she must do something to provide her audience access to her two intentions and the different properties they determine; and that she must make clear to her audience which intention is associated with which occurrence of the 'that' phrase. This claim is supported by the fact that in examples of NDNS uses with nonredundant intentions, such as our examples (15)–(17) above, where a 'that' phrase occurs only once in a sentence, demonstrations are not necessary.[31]

Turning to QI uses, we find exactly the same sort of data supporting the claim that there are nonredundant intentions in some cases. Taking the simpler case first, suppose some friends and I are watching a scene in a movie in which a professor is fondly flipping through what is being depicted as his finest piece of published work. I say to my friends,

(19)   Every professor cherishes that publication of his.

Presumably, in using the 'that' phrase I intend to talk about the unique instance of being x's finest publication, for every professor x. So my intention determines the relation *y is the finest publication of x*.[32] Thus I express a proposition to the effect that every professor x cherishes the unique instance y of being x's finest publication. As in the NDNS cases, speakers who wish to be understood will only have nonredundant intentions in QI uses where something gives their audience access to their intentions. Here it is the shared experience of watching the movie that performs this role.

Again, substituting an exactly similar description for the 'that' phrase in (19) results in infelicity:

*(19a)   Every professor cherishes the publication of his.

And again, I claim that this is because the description is radically incomplete and its semantics doesn't allow for supplementation by a property/relation determined by the speaker's intentions. Since the semantics of the 'that' phrase does allow for such supplementation, and since the supplementation is semantically significant in this case, (19) is fine.

Consider a second example. Suppose that when a race car driver wins a certain number of races, he is automatically inducted into the prestigious Checkered Flag Club. We are watching the end of a race in which the winning driver has, in virtue of this very win, achieved that mark. Intending to convey how important the Checkered Flag Club is to race car drivers, I say:

(20)   Every race car driver with many, many victories under his belt still remembers that race he won.

Presumably my intentions determine the relation *y is the victory that gave x enough victories to be inducted into the Checkered Flag Club*. As such, in uttering (20) I express a proposition to the effect that for every race car driver with many, many victories *x*, *x* still remembers the unique instance *y* of being the victory that gave *x* enough victories to be inducted into the Checkered Flag Club. Again, the crucial point is that substituting a definite description for the 'that' phrase here results in oddness:

*(20a)   Every race car driver with many, many victories under his belt still remembers the race he won.

Turning to the more complex case, suppose we are now watching two movies simultaneously. On one screen (to the left) is the scene described before, with a professor flipping through his finest publication. On the other screen (to the right) is a scene in which a professor is disgustedly flipping through his *poorest* publication. I say to my friends:

(21)   Every professor cherishes that publication of his [nodding to the left] but not that publication of his [nodding to the right].

As in the similar NDNS case, since I associate different intentions with the two occurrences of the 'that' phrase and these determine two different properties, to be understood I must provide my audience access to my intentions and the properties they determine and I must make clear which intentions are associated with which occurrences of the 'that' phrase. I do this by nodding, thereby exploiting the film we are watching. The intention associated with the first occurrence of the 'that' phrase determines the relation *y is x's finest publication*; and the intention associated with the second occurrence of the 'that' phrase determines the relation *z is x's poorest publication*. Thus, (21) expresses a proposition that is true iff every professor cherishes his finest publication but does not cherish his poorest publication.[33] As before, we note that substituting exactly similar definite descriptions leads to infelicity:

*(21a)   Every professor cherishes the publication of his [nodding to the left] but not the publication of his [nodding to the right].

And as before, we hold that this constitutes evidence that the speaker's intentions are not redundant in (21).[34]

When one looks at the data comprised by examples (15)–(21), one is struck by the fact that 'that' phrases in NDNS and QI uses exhibit precisely the same differences in behavior from definite descriptions as they do in classic demonstrative uses. In all these uses, we have examples where a sentence containing a single 'that' phrase is felicitous but in which substitution of an exactly similar definite description yields oddness or infelicity ('I wish I could ski like that skier'; (15); (16); (17); (19); (20)). And we have more complex examples in which a sentence contains two 'that' phrases that are being used to talk about different things, where substitution of exactly similar definite descriptions yields infelicity ('That car is nicer than that car'; (18); (21)). For now, I simply wish to note that 'that' phrases behave differently from definite descriptions *in the same way* in classic demonstrative uses, NDNS uses, and QI uses. I shall return to this fact in chapter 5.

One final point before turning to other matters. In the cases discussed so far, the speakers' intentions in QI uses, whether redundant or not, have been descriptive. However, I think there are examples of QI uses in which a speaker has a (nonredundant) *perceptual intention*. In such a case, given what was said earlier, since the intention is perceptual, the 'that' phrase ought to be rigid. And this indeed seems correct. An example would be one in which I am in front of an exclusive club and many people are trying to get in. As I form the intention to talk about a man in the crowd, I point at him and say to the doorman:

(22)   The owner of the club wants that friend of his to be let in.

Here my perceptual intention determines *both* the property of being identical to b, where b is the man in question, *and* the property of pairs of properties of *being jointly instantiated in w,t*, where *w,t* are the world and time of the context of my utterance. Thus the use of the 'that' phrase will be rigid, and the truth of the proposition expressed at an arbitrary circumstance of evaluation *e* will require that in *e* the owner of the club wants the very man demonstrated in the context of utterance to be let into the club. Intuitively, this seems exactly correct. That QI uses of 'that' phrases are rigid when used with perceptual intentions and not when used with descriptive intentions, just as our theory predicts, constitutes significant confirmation of our theory.

Let me summarize the present theory's treatment of the various examples we have looked at in this chapter. First, we saw how the present view accounts for the facts about rigidity that have been used to motivate a direct reference account. Second, the application to NDNS uses illustrated cases in which speaker intentions are redundant. Third, we saw other NDNS cases in which speaker intentions were not redundant. We noted that NDNS cases always involve descriptive intentions on the part of the speaker and so, barring very unusual cases, are nonrigid whether speaker intentions are redundant or not.[35] Fourth, QI uses again illustrated cases involving redundant intentions, and also showed that speaker intentions sometimes determine relations rather than properties. Further, we saw that in QI cases, speaker intentions can be descriptive or perceptual. When they are descriptive, they may or may not be redundant. But in either case, the uses are nonrigid. When QI uses are accompanied by perceptual intentions, the intentions are not redundant (barring very unusual cases) and the uses are rigid. Finally, in discussing QI and NDNS uses with nonredundant intentions, we noted that 'that' phrases behave differently from definite descriptions in such cases *in the same way* they do in classic demonstrative uses.

There are two final points that merit at least a brief comment. The first concerns the properties determined by speakers' intentions. We have said that when a speaker has a perceptual intention, her intention determines both the property of being identical to b (where b is the object of the intention) and the property of being jointly instantiated in w,t (where w,t are the world and time of the context of utterance). By contrast, we claimed that when a speaker has a descriptive intention, the speaker's intention determines what we called the property of the descriptive intention and the property of being jointly instantiated. That the speaker's intentions determine the property of being jointly instantiated in w,t in the one case and being jointly instantiated in the other is the reason that utterances of 'That F is G' with perceptual intentions express propositions whose truth at an arbitrary world w' doesn't require b (the object of the intention) to possess the property expressed by 'F' at w' (though their truth at w' does require b to possess this property at w,t—the world and time of the context of utterance). In contrast, utterances of 'That F is G' with descriptive intentions express propositions whose truth at an arbitrary world w' require something to possess the property expressed by 'F' (and the property determined by the speaker's intentions) at w'. We also claimed that when a speaker has a perceptual intention, the speaker intends to talk about b and is using the predicate 'F' to pick out b in the context of utterance in such a case. Thus, the speaker intends to express a proposition that tracks b across worlds and times, regardless of its possession of the property expressed by 'F' at those worlds and times. This is why the speaker's intentions determine the property of being jointly instantiated in w,t in such cases. When a speaker uses a 'that' phrase without a perceptual intention, however, there is no particular thing she intends to talk about. Thus, we claimed, she is not concerned to express a proposition that tracks a particular object across worlds and times regardless of its possession of the property expressed by 'F'. Thus, her intentions determine the property of being jointly instantiated.

To summarize, then, we have assumed that having what we called *a descriptive intention*, an intention to talk about whatever satisfies a certain conjunction of properties C, goes along with not intending to make a claim that tracks a particular object across worlds and times, and so such an intention determines (C and) the property of being jointly instantiated. And we have assumed that having what we called *a perceptual intention* whose object is b, an intention to talk about an object b one is perceiving, goes along with intending to make a claim that tracks b across worlds and times regardless of what properties it possesses, and so such an intention determines (being identical to b and) the property of being jointly instantiated in w,t (where w,t are the world and time of the context of one's utterance).

However, it might be thought that we were too hasty here. Why couldn't a speaker have an intention to "talk about" whatever uniquely satisfies some conjunction of properties C, but still intend to express a proposition that tracks the thing satisfying C *in the actual world* across worlds and times regardless of whether it possesses C at these other worlds and times? If this were possible, the speaker's intention in such a case would determine C and the property of being jointly instantiated in w,t (where w,t are the world and time of the speaker's context of utterance). A 'that' phrase used with such an intention in w,t would be rigid and would "pick out" in every possible world the object satisfying the properties of the descriptive intention (C) and the property expressed by the predicative material in the 'that' phrase in w,t.[36]

Similarly, we might allow that a speaker, in uttering 'That F is G', may use the 'that' phrase with the intention to talk about some object she is perceiving, say b, but *not* intend to make a claim that tracks b across times and worlds regardless of its possession of the property expressed by 'F'. In such a case, we might suppose that her intention determines the property of being identical to b and the property of being jointly instantiated (rather than being jointly instantiated in w,t, where w,t are the world and time of her context of utterance). If this were so, the speaker's utterance of 'That F is G' in such a case would express a proposition whose truth at an arbitrary world w' would require b to possess the properties expressed by 'F' and 'G' *at* w' (rather than requiring b to possess the property expressed by 'F' *at* w,t—the world and time of the context of utterance).

If, in addition to the sorts of intentions we until now claimed speakers have in using 'that' phrases, they may have intentions of the sorts just described, then speakers may have any one of *four* kinds of intentions in using 'that' phrases. A speaker uttering 'That F is G' in w,t may intend:

(i) to talk about an object b she is perceiving and make a claim that tracks b across worlds and times regardless of b's possessing the property expressed by 'F' at those worlds and times. In this case, her intention determines the property of being identical to b and being jointly instantiated in w,t.

(ii) to talk about an object b she is perceiving and *not* make a claim that tracks b across worlds and times regardless of b's possessing the property expressed by 'F' at those worlds and times. In this case, her intention determines the property of being identical to b and being jointly instantiated.

(iii) to talk about whatever satisfies some conjunction of properties Q and *not* to make a claim that tracks whatever satisfies Q at w,t across worlds and times regardless of whether it possesses Q at them. In this case, her intention determines Q and the property of being jointly instantiated.

(iv) to talk about whatever satisfies some conjunction of properties Q and to make a claim that tracks whatever satisfies Q at w,t across worlds and times regardless of whether it possesses Q at them. In this case, her intention determines Q and the property of being jointly instantiated at w,t.

Additions, complications, and adjustments would have to be made to (i)–(iv) to accommodate QI uses, in which speaker intentions typically determine relations rather than properties.

'That' phrases used with intentions of the sort (i), (ii), and (iv) would be rigid; those used with intentions of sort (iii) would not be. One obvious difference between this account and our original account is that the category we called *NDNS uses* would divide up into two categories on the present formulation. For we assumed that in NDNS uses, since the speaker had an intention to talk about whatever satisfies some conjunction of properties Q, her intention also determined the property of being jointly instantiated and so was always of sort (iii). But now we are considering allowing intentions of sort (iv). Thus some uses in which the speaker has an intention to talk about whatever satisfies some conjunction of properties Q (and so would have been called *NDNS uses*) could involve intentions of the sort (iii) (and so be nonrigid); and some could involve intentions of sort (iv) (and so be rigid). We might envisage a similar ramification of the category we called *QI uses* (though see below).

Having come this far, it should be clear that our original account that allowed only two sorts of intentions (perceptual and descriptive) and the present account that allows four sorts of intentions (see (i)–(iv) above) are two endpoints of a spectrum of accounts. The original account claims that the properties that (in a given use of a 'that' phrase) saturate the second argument place in the four-place relation expressed by 'that' (and so restrict the range of the quantification expressed) and the properties of being jointly instantiated in w,t and being jointly instantiated are *not* determined independently. If a speaker's intention determines a property like being identical to b, it determines being jointly instantiated in w,t. And if it determines some other sort of property or conjunction of properties, it determines being jointly instantiated. Hence this account claims that speakers' intentions in using 'that' phrases determine either of the following pairs of properties (where

Q is a conjunction of properties of the sort we claimed are determined by what we called *descriptive intentions*): $\langle=$b, jointly instantiated in $w,t\rangle$; $\langle Q$, jointly instantiated$\rangle$.

By contrast, the account that posits (i)–(iv) (and whatever is required for QI uses that involve either the property of being jointly instantiated or the property of being jointly instantiated in w,t) claims that the property that saturates the second argument place in the four-place relation expressed by 'that' and the properties of being jointly instantiated and being jointly instantiated in w,t are determined completely independently, in that a speaker's intention may determine *any* of the following property pairs (where Q is a conjunction of properties of the sort we claimed are determined by what we called *descriptive intentions*): $\langle=$b, jointly instantiated in $w,t\rangle$; $\langle=$b, jointly instantiated$\rangle$; $\langle Q$, jointly instantiated in $w,t\rangle$; $\langle Q$, jointly instantiated$\rangle$.

But we can imagine intermediate views according to which speakers in using 'that' phrases simply don't have intentions that determine certain pairings, but in which more pairings than the original two occur. Perhaps one rejects intentions of type (ii) because one thinks (as I tend to) that whenever one utters 'That F is G' with a perceptual intention whose object is b, one intends to track b across worlds and time regardless of its possession of the property expressed by 'F'. Thus, in such a case one's intention always determines the property of being jointly instantiated in w,t, so that the pairing $\langle=$b, jointly instantiated$\rangle$ is ruled out. Or perhaps one thinks that QI uses involving descriptive intentions are never rigid (as I tend to), so that one thinks that when a speaker has an intention that determines a *relation*, it always also determines the property of being jointly instantiated. Here again, certain pairs of properties would be ruled out as not being determined by intentions of the sort people have in using 'that' phrases. For what it is worth, my current inclination is to think that *either* our original account, which allowed only two sorts of intentions, *or* an account that adds only a third sort of intention corresponding to (iv) above (and so holds that what our original account calls *NDNS uses* divide up into what we might call *rigid* and *nonrigid NDNS* uses) is correct.

In any case, as we have seen, the theories under discussion differ in terms of how many kinds of intentions speakers have in using 'that' phrases. Determining which of these theories is correct would require painstaking consideration of a lot of complex and subtle data, and so I leave this question open at present.[37] However, for the remainder of this work (except briefly in chapter 5), I shall talk as though our original theory that posits two sorts of intentions is correct.

The second point I wish to discuss before closing this chapter concerns the formulation of the theory. As I have formulated the theory, the lexical meaning of 'that' (what it expresses "outside of any context") is a four-place relation. When 'that' is used in a given context, properties determined by the speaker's intentions saturate two of the arguments places in the four-place relation it expresses. The resulting two-place relation is contributed to the proposition expressed by the sentence containing the 'that' phrase. Thus, on the present view, generally in different contexts with speakers whose intentions are different, 'that' will contribute different two-place relations between properties to propositions. It is in this sense that 'that' is contextually sensitive on the present view. Now the view could be formulated in a slightly different way. 'That' could have as its lexical meaning a function f from pairs of properties (determined by the speaker's intention) to determiner denotations (two-place relations between properties). The function f would be a (nonconstant) character-like (in Kaplan's sense) semantic value. The contextual sensitivity of 'that' would consist in the fact that f is not a constant function. Such a formulation would not commit us to the claim that the meaning of 'that' is a four-place relation some of whose argument places are saturated by properties determined by the speaker's intentions. On the formulation we have chosen, we are of course committed to the claim that the meaning of 'that' is such a relation. This relation in turn *determines* the function from pairs of properties (determined by the speaker's intentions) to determiner denotations (two-place relations between properties) that the alternative formulation puts forth as the semantic value of 'that'. The advantages of this latter formulation over the one we have chosen and vice versa shall not be discussed here. I simply note that the theory could be formulated in this alternative fashion.[38]

3   *Modality, Negation, and Verbs of Propositional*

Attitude

Having sketched the basic features of the quantificational
account of 'that' phrases I favor, I can now consider more
complex data. More specifically, since I claim that 'that'
phrases are quantificational, like other quantifiers they
should engage in scope interactions with other elements
that have scope. Thus, we need to look at constructions in
which 'that' phrases combine with other elements that have
scope to see whether they exhibit quantifier-like behavior.
In particular, we would like to see evidence of *narrow*
scope readings of 'that' phrases with respect to various
scoped elements. For these are the readings that cannot be
accounted for by direct reference theorists and so support
the view that 'that' phrases are quantificational.

It is worth remarking that both QI uses and NS readings of sentences are cases in which 'that' phrases, qua
quantifiers, take narrow scope with respect to other quantifiers. And, of course, it is precisely the fact that the 'that'
phrases in such cases *do* behave semantically like quantifiers taking narrow scope with respect to other quantifiers
that causes the direct reference theorist trouble. So we
already have *some* evidence that 'that' phrases exhibit
the sorts of variable scope relations that other quantifiers
do.

However, we must look at how 'that' phrases interact with scoped elements other than other quantifiers.[1] In considering particular examples, it is important to specify whether the 'that' phrase is being used with perceptual or descriptive intentions, since, as we have seen, this has a significant effect on the contribution the 'that' phrase makes to the proposition expressed by the sentence in which it occurs. Considerations of space (and tediousness!) preclude our considering each sort of use of a 'that' phrase in combination with each sort of other scoped element. We will, however, consider enough combinations to give a good sense of the predictions and plausibility of our theory. As I said above, we will be especially concerned with narrow scope readings of 'that' phrases with respect to other scoped elements. Because we have already discussed some examples of modal operators combining with 'that' phrases, we begin our discussion with the interaction of 'that' phrases and modality.

In chapter 2, we considered the sentence

(1) It is possible that that senator from California is a crook

(i.e., it is possible that that senator from California should have been a crook), uttered as I point at a man, b, sitting in the corner of a bar. My perceptual intention determines the property of *being identical to b* in such a case, and my theory predicted that (1) has the following two readings in the situation as described:

(1a) [[THAT$_{=b, Jwt}$ senator from California: x] [Possibly [x is a crook]]]

(1b) [Possibly [[THAT$_{=b, Jwt}$ senator from California: x] [x is a crook]]]

where w, t are the world and time of the context of utterance and THAT$_{=b, Jwt}$ is the two-place relation resulting from saturating the second and third argument places of the four-place relation expressed by 'that' with the properties of *being identical to* b and *being jointly instantiated in w,t*, respectively. We noted that if we confine our attention to worlds in which b exists, (1a) and (1b) will not diverge in truth value. So even though we claim there is a scope ambiguity in (1), subject to the assumptions we have made this ambiguity is truth-conditionally inert.

However, (1a) and (1b) can diverge in truth value *if* we consider worlds where b doesn't exist. In particular, (1a) could not be true at a world w' where b doesn't exist, because there would be nothing in the domain of that world that is identical to b and a senator from California in w,t.[2] By contrast, (1b) *could* be true in a world w' in which b doesn't exist. If b exists in some world w'' possible relative to w' and is a crook there, (1b) is true at w' (assuming b is a senator from California in w,t—the world and time of the context of utterance).

Though my theory predicts that (1) can express two different propositions in the situation as described, and though these propositions can diverge in truth value in worlds in which b fails to exist, I believe our intuitions about truth and falsity in such cases are sufficiently weak that we cannot tell whether this prediction is correct. Certainly it is not clearly incorrect. And the theory's claim that (1) does not have readings that can diverge in truth value at worlds where b exists *does* seem clearly correct.

Let us now turn to the combination of NDNS uses of 'that' phrases and modal operators. For the sake of simplicity, we shall assume that speakers' intentions are redundant in the cases we consider.[3] Suppose I am looking at a friend's data on biomass production in a certain ecosystem. There are two types of plants in the ecosystem. The other day my friend walked through two plots, pulling approximately equal numbers of the two types of plants from each plot, and pulling seven plants from each plot. The type A plants have much more biomass than the type B plants. She notes that the total biomass recorded in plot one is significantly larger than in plot two. Looking at her data, I note that she pulled four of seven type A plants from plot one and three of seven type A plants from plot two. Finally, I note that her data show that the last plant she pulled from plot two was type B, and I note that she was pretty random about pulling the plants (sometimes pulling two type A plants from a row, etc.). Not having seen any of the plants she pulled, and so having no particular plants in mind, I say:

(2)   It is possible that that last plant you pulled from plot two should have been type A instead of type B. In that case the total biomass for the two plots would have been almost identical and you would have had equal numbers of type A and type B plants from both plots.[4]

Intuitively, the first sentence of (2) seems true in the situation as described, where my friend is picking plants fairly randomly. It does seem possible that she should have picked a type A plant last instead of a type B plant. In principle, the first sentence of (2) ought to have two readings corresponding to the 'that' phrase taking wide and narrow scope with respect to the modal operator. These readings could be presented as follows:

(2a)   [THAT$_{I,J}$ last plant you pulled from plot two: x] [Possibly [x is type A instead of type B]]

(2b)   Possibly [[THAT$_{I,J}$ last plant you pulled from plot two: x] [x is type A instead of type B]]

(where THAT$_{I,J}$ is the result of saturating the second and third argument places in the four-place relation expressed by 'that' with the property of being the last plant my friend pulled from plot two [l—since my intentions were redundant] and the property of being jointly instantiated (J)). But now (2a) is false in the situation described. Concerning the plant that was in fact picked last and is type B, it is presumably *not* metaphysically possible that the plant should have been type A. And in any case, if we interpret the initial sentence as (2a), it doesn't make sense of the continuation. The continuation presupposes that the first sentence invites us to consider a possible world in which *the last plant picked in that world* was type A (and everything else remained the same). (2a) invites us to consider a possibility in which what was *in fact* the last plant picked is type A; but it need not be the last plant picked *in the possibility being considered*. Since the first sentence of (2) seems both true and relevant to the continuation in the situation as described, it must have the reading (2b). The reading corresponding to (2b) seems true: it seems metaphysically possible that my friend should have picked a type A plant last instead of a type B plant. Further, the reading corresponding to (2b) proposes a possibility that makes sense of the continuation, since the reading proposes a possibility in which the last plant picked was type A.[5]

Consider a second example of an NDNS use taking narrow scope with respect to a modal operator. Scott is picking numbers at random and writing down his choices. After he records a choice, Greg and I bet on whether the number is odd or even. Once we place our bets, Scott tells us whether the number chosen is odd or even, but does not tell us the number. After a series of bets, Greg and I are dead even. We decide to place one more bet. Greg bets that the number is odd and loses. We are never told what number was selected. Later, someone tells Greg he made a bad choice on the last bet. Greg responds, not knowing what number was chosen last and so having no particular number in mind,

(3) Look, it is possible that that last number Scott picked should have been odd instead of even.

Intuitively, Greg's utterance seems true. But clearly the reading corresponding to (2a), where the 'that' phrase takes wide scope over the modal operator, is false. Concerning the number Scott in fact picked last, say, 4, it is not possible that it should have been odd. By contrast, the reading corresponding to (2b), where the 'that' phrase takes narrow scope with respect to the modal operator, is true. Since Greg's utterance seems true here, it must have the reading corresponding to (2b). So again we have an NDNS use taking narrow scope with respect to a modal operator.[6]

I have gone through these examples (particularly the first) in some detail to make clear to the reader that NDNS uses of 'that' phrases really do take narrow scope with respect to modal operators. Of course they can take wide scope too, and here we can be more brief. Consider Ranger Scott, who knows on general grounds that exactly one person was climbing El Capitan on Wednesday, having deduced this from information about climbing permits issued, the amount of time it takes to climb El Capitan, and so on. Ranger Scott, without anyone in mind and knowing the difficulties one can encounter in preparing for a serious climb, says truly:

(4) It is possible that that person climbing El Capitan on Wednesday should not have been climbing El Capitan on Wednesday.

Again, in principle (4) has two readings:

(4a) [THAT$_{p,J}$ person climbing El Capitan on Wednesday: x] [Possibly [x didn't climb El Capitan on Wednesday]]

(4b) Possibly [[THAT$_{p,J}$ person climbing El Capitan on Wednesday: x] [x didn't climb El Capitan on Wednesday]] (where THAT$_{p,J}$ is the result of saturating the second and third arguments in the four-place relation expressed by 'that' with the properties of being a person climbing El Capitan on Wednesday and being jointly instantiated, respectively). (4b), of course, is false. But intuitively, Ranger Scott spoke truly. And (4a) is true in the situation described: concerning the person who in fact climbed El Capitan Wednesday, he might not have. So here the 'that' phrase takes wide scope with respect to the modal operator. Thus, my theory predicts correctly that NDNS uses of 'that' phrases can take wide or narrow scope with respect to modal operators, and such scope differences make truth-conditional differences.

It is exceedingly easy to get narrow scope readings of QI uses with respect to modal operators.[7] Certainly, the most natural reading of:

(5)   It is possible that every professor cherishes that first publication of his/hers

is given by

(5a)   Possibly [[every professor: x] [THAT$_{Fx,y,J}$ first publication of x's: y] [x cherishes y]],

where THAT$_{Fx,y,J}$ is the result of saturating the second and third argument places in the four-place relation expressed by 'that' with the relation y is the first publication of x (Fx,y), and the property of being jointly instantiated (J), respectively. (5a) is true (in the actual world) iff there is a world w' such that in w' every professor cherishes his or her unique first publication.[8]

It is difficult (though I think not impossible) to find examples in which QI uses of 'that' phrases are clearly and naturally read as taking wide scope over modal operators. I shall not bother with trying to construct such examples, because here 'that' phrases behave as do other quantifier phrases in any case. In a sentence in which one quantifier phrase binds variables in another and the entire sentence is embedded with respect to a modal operator, as in

(6) It is possible that every man loves some woman he kissed,

(on one of its readings), it is very difficult to read the sentence in such a way that both quantifiers take wide scope over the modal operator.[9] Thus the fact that such readings are hard to get for QI uses of 'that' phrases simply shows that in this respect they behave like other quantifiers. Further, as already mentioned, we are more concerned to show that 'that' phrases can take *narrow* scope with respect to other scoped elements, and this is what we have in the reading of (5) corresponding to (5a).

Let us now turn our attention to the interaction of 'that' phrases and negation. Because cases of this sort involving perceptual intentions raise a host of difficult issues, let us begin with the somewhat simpler case of NDNS uses. As in the modal case, when considering scope interactions in these uses nonredundant intentions introduce complexity without making any difference, and so we again assume intentions are redundant in the cases we consider. Because we continue to do this, I remind the reader that there *are* cases exactly like those we shall consider, except that intentions are not redundant.

We begin by considering in the abstract the two propositions that in principle can be expressed by a sentence containing an NDNS use of a 'that' phrase and negation. So imagine that a speaker utters 'That F is not G', where her intentions determine the property F^*, which is also expressed by the predicate 'F', making her intentions redundant. The two propositions she may express by her utterance can be represented as:

(7a) $[\text{THAT}_{F^*,J}\ F^*: x]\ [\text{Not}\ [x\ \text{is}\ G^*]]$

(7b) $\text{Not}\ [[\text{THAT}_{F^*,J}\ F^*: x]\ [x\ \text{is}\ G^*]]$,

where $\text{THAT}_{F^*,J}$ is the four-place relation expressed by 'that' with the second and third argument places saturated by F^* and the property of being jointly instantiated (J), respectively. These propositions have significantly different truth conditions. (7a) is true at a world w iff in w, F^* and F^* are uniquely jointly instantiated in an object x and x is not G^* in w. (7b) is true at w, by contrast, iff in w the following is not the case: F^* and F^* are uniquely jointly instantiated in an object x and x is G^* in w. Thus the truth of (7a) at w requires F^* to have a unique instance there, and requires the instance not to be G^* there. Whereas the truth of (7b) at w requires *either* that F^* has no unique instance at w *or* that it has one, and that this instance fails to be G^*.

It is certainly easy to find NDNS uses in sentences of the form 'That F is not G' that seem to have the truth conditions of (7a). For example, consider again Ranger Scott who believes on general grounds that exactly one person climbed El Capitan on Wednesday. Further, Ranger Scott believes this climber was not struck by the chunk of exfoliated granite that tumbled down El Capitan that day. Ranger Scott says:

(8)   That person climbing El Capitan on Wednesday was not struck by a chunk of granite.

In such a case, it does not seem that the mere failure of there to have been a unique person climbing El Capitan on Wednesday suffices for the truth of Scott's utterance. For Ranger Scott to have spoken truly, it seems that there must have been a unique person climbing El Capitan on Wednesday who was not struck by a chunk of granite. Thus, (8) in such a case seems to have the reading corresponding to (7a). Similar examples are readily produced. Indeed, one might start to wonder whether one can produce examples of NDNS uses in sentences of the form 'That F is not G' where the sentences have the reading corresponding instead to (7b). In such examples, there being no unique F would suffice for truth. If such examples cannot be produced, one might well claim that this is a strike against the present theory, which does seem to predict that sentences of the form 'That F is not G' containing NDNS uses have readings corresponding to (7b).

There are two points to make in response to this concern. First, in some range of cases, we do seem to be able to get the readings corresponding to (7b). And second, that it is difficult to get these readings does not cut against the view that 'that' phrases are quantificational. I begin by giving a few examples to illustrate the first point.

Egomaniacal Alan always tries to impress people, and is prone to making false claims in attempting to do so. Alan has claimed to several of us that yesterday a supermodel approached him and told him he was extremely handsome. Knowing Alan, we don't believe him and we are correct not to. At noon the next day, we drive by Alan's house and see someone other than Alan inside. Someone wonders who it could be. I comment that I don't know, and I then say,

(9) At any rate, that supermodel who told Alan he is handsome isn't in there.

I have a strong tendency to hear this as true, if in fact no supermodel told Alan he was handsome yesterday. But then presumably, it must have the reading corresponding to (7b). Thus, the 'that' phrase here appears to take narrow scope with respect to negation.

Though our primary concern at present is scope interactions between negation and 'that' phrases, it is worth digressing briefly and considering scope interactions between 'that' phrases and *monotone decreasing* quantifiers. For the example we are considering brings out readings on which 'that' phrases take narrow scope with respect to such quantifiers. So here again, we have evidence of 'that' phrases taking narrow scope with respect to other elements that have scope.

A determiner D is *monotone decreasing* iff

DA is B

and

Every C is B

entail

DA is C.

A *quantifier* is monotone decreasing iff it is formed using a monotone descreasing determiner. Paradigmatic monotone decreasing quantifiers are those formed using the determiner 'no'. Thus, that 'No student is six feet tall' and 'Every blond is six feet tall' entail 'No student is blond' shows that 'No', and hence 'No student', is monotone decreasing. Similarly, of course, for other quantifiers formed using the determiner 'no'. Thinking of our example above involving Alan, suppose that instead of (9) I utter:

(10)   Funny, no person in town has seen that supermodel who told Alan he is handsome.

Because of the scope ambiguity involving the quantifiers in (10), it has two readings, which can be represented as follows (leaving off 'Funny'):

(10a)   [No person in town: x] [[that supermodel who told Alan he is handsome: y] [x has seen y]]

(10b)   [that supermodel who told Alan he is handsome: y] [[No person in town: x] [x has seen y]]

(10a) and (10b) have different truth conditions. (10a) is true iff nothing *both* is a person in this town *and* has seen a unique instance of being a supermodel who told Alan he is handsome. (10b) is true iff being a supermodel who told Alan he is handsome has a unique instance y and no one in this town has seen y. Thus, the truth of (10b) requires there to be a (unique) supermodel who told Alan he is handsome, whereas the truth of (10a) does not. The important point is that in the situation as described, in which no supermodel told Alan he is handsome, (10) does seem to have a true reading. But then this must be the reading corresponding to (10a). Thus, here we have evidence that the 'that' phrase takes narrow scope with respect to the monotone decreasing quantifier 'no person in this town'.

Returning now to NDNS uses of 'that' phrases and negation, let's consider another example. Suppose Mary's son Chris believes that a monster lives in his closet. The monster, he believes, is fairly well behaved most of the time. However, lately he believes that the monster is restless and intent on scaring and harassing him. In particular, he believes that every time Mary turns off the light in his room, the monster hides under his bed. After many attempts at getting her son to go to sleep, an exasperated Mary says:

(11) That monster of yours is not under your bed.

Again, even if, as seems likely, there is no monster, I am inclined to think that Mary spoke truly. So here again, the sentence seems to have the reading corresponding to (7b).

I also note that here again we get a true reading of a sentence containing a monotone decreasing quantifier and the relevant 'that' phrase. Suppose Mary says to Chris:

(12) No member of this family other than you has seen that monster of yours.

Again, this seems true. But then this reading of the sentence must correspond to the reading (10a) on which the 'that' phrase takes narrow scope with respect to the monotone decreasing quantifier.

There is a final phenomenon that suggests that NDNS uses may take narrow scope with respect to negation. Suppose that young Alice believes on general grounds that exactly one student at her school can fly, without having any view about which student it is. Alice's views on this matter are well known among her fellow students and the school staff. Poor Alice, as might be expected, is mistaken. One day in taking role at an assembly meeting of the entire school, the mean principal of the school attempts some humor at Alice's expense and says:

(13)   That student who can fly is not present today.

Again, this seems to have a true reading. This, of course, would require negation to take wide scope over the 'that' phrase on the reading in question. But, more importantly, consider the contrast between (13) and (13'):

(13')   That student who can fly is absent today.

Given that there is no flying student, it is very hard to hear (13') as true. In that sense, there is a significant contrast between (13) and (13'). Indeed, even if one has a hard time hearing (13) as true, I submit that it is much harder to hear (13') as true. But one would think that 'is not present today' and 'is absent today' would (at least in the context described) predicate more or less the same thing of an individual. Thus, it is hard to see how to explain the tendency to hear (13) as having a true reading and not hear (13') this way in the case as described except by saying that in (13) there is an occurrence of 'not' for the 'that' phrase to take narrow scope with respect to, and not in (13') (where the "negative element" is "built into" the semantics of 'absent'). Thus the contrast between (13) and (13′) again provides evidence that 'that' phrases in NDNS uses may take narrow scope with respect to negation.[10]

Some will think that these uses are odd or perhaps just not typical. They will claim that the fact that we can't get readings corresponding to (7b) easily and more straightforwardly in a wider range of cases casts doubt on the present account. But I think this is incorrect. For we find an exactly similar phenomenon in the case of definite descriptions. And here philosophers of language overwhelmingly agree that the expressions in question are quantifiers. Notoriously, contra Russell, the lack of a unique male monarch of France does not seem to many to suffice for the truth of

(14)   The present King of France is not bald.

Thus, in such examples it is hard to read the description as taking narrow scope with respect to negation.[11] However, as many have noticed, one can get uses of sentences of the form 'The F is not G' where the lack of a unique F seems to suffice for their truth, and so the description is read as taking narrow scope. For example, suppose I comment to my dining companions:

(14′)   The present King of France is not under this table.

Here, as in the cases involving Alan and Mary above, there is a strong tendency to think I have spoken truly. So this behavior is extremely similar to that exhibited by 'that' phrases. For both 'that' phrases and definite descriptions, readings on which they take narrow scope relative to negation are present only in certain examples. Thus if we still hold that definite descriptions are quantificational in light of such behavior, we should not let this behavior count against the view that 'that' phrases are quantificational.[12]

With respect to scope interactions between QI uses and negation, I shall be fairly brief, again relying on the fact that 'that' phrases behave similarly to definite descriptions. I continue to assume for simplicity that we are dealing with cases in which speaker intentions are redundant. Let us begin by looking at definite descriptions. Consider

(15)   Every man does not love the first woman he kissed.

On the reading we are interested in, 'Every man' binds the pronoun 'he' in the definite description 'the first woman he kissed', and so takes wide scope over the description. In principle, this leaves three possible scope arrangements between the quantifiers and negation. These can be represented as follows:

(15a)   [[Every man: x] [[the first woman x kissed: y]
[Not [x loves y]]]]

(15b)   [[Every man: x] Not [[the first woman x kissed: y]
[x loves y]]]

(15c)   Not [[Every man: x] [[the first woman x kissed: y]
[x loves y]]]

My feeling is that the first of these readings is the most natural for (15), even though, being likely false, it is not favored on pragmatic grounds.[13] This reading is true iff for every man x and the first woman x kissed, y, x fails to love y. In particular, then, the truth of the sentence on this reading requires there to be for every man, a unique woman he kissed first. Now does (15) have readings corresponding to (15b) and (15c)? On the one hand, in part because of the unlikelihood of (15a)'s being true, there is a tendency to hear (15) as having a reading that in some sense is the denial of the claim that every man loves the first woman he kissed. Let us call this reading, whose truth conditions have not yet been completely delineated, D.

Heard on D, the failure of some man to love the first woman he kissed suffices for the truth of (15). And, of course, this would suffice for the truth of (15c). (15c), however, would also be true if for some man, there failed to be a unique woman he first kissed. But I tend to hear D as requiring that for every man, there is a unique woman he first kissed, and then requiring that some man fails to love the unique woman he first kissed. (15c), of course, does not require this. So it isn't *clear* that D corresponds to (15c), nor is it clear that it doesn't.[14]

(15b)'s truth requires that for every man, either there is no unique first woman he kissed or there is and he fails to love her. It is unclear to me whether (15) has this reading. But in any case, it doesn't capture the reading D. For as we have said, it suffices for the truth of D that some man fails to love the first woman he kissed, but this doesn't suffice for the truth of (15b).

So the situation here seems to be this. (15) (understood with the pronoun 'he' bound by the quantifier 'Every man') has a reading corresponding to (15a). It also *seems* to have a reading that in some sense is the denial of the claim that every man loves the first woman he kissed. It isn't entirely clear that this reading corresponds to (15c), though it may. Further, it also is not clear that (15) has a reading corresponding to (15b), though even if it does, it is not the reading D.

For our purposes, the important point is that similar sentences involving 'that' phrases instead of definite descriptions exhibit the same behavior. Consider

(16)   Every father does not look forward to that moment when his oldest child leaves home.

As with (15), (16) seems clearly to have a reading on which both 'Every father' and 'that moment ...' take wide scope over negation. Further, (16), like (15), *seems* to have a reading on which it is in some sense the denial of the claim that every father looks forward to that moment when his oldest child leaves home. But here again, it is not clear that this reading corresponds to the analogue of (15c). For it does not seem that the fact that there is a father all of whose children never leave home (so that there is no moment when his oldest child leaves) suffices for the truth of the reading in question, though it would suffice for the truth of the analogue of (15c). And, again, it is not clear that (16) has a reading corresponding to the analogue of (15b). So QI uses interact with negation in ways that are exactly similar to the ways in which definite descriptions containing pronouns bound by "higher" quantifiers interact with negation. Thus, if we think that definite descriptions are quantificational, the data involving QI uses of 'that' phrases and negation cannot possibly undermine, and in fact support, the claim that 'that' phrases are quantificational.

Finally, we turn to the most complex cases: those involving a 'that' phrase used with a perceptual intention, combined with negation. Imagine that a speaker at world w and time t has a perceptual intention whose object is b, and says:

(17)   That F is not G.

On the present view, since the 'that' phrase is a quantifier, in principle there are two possible scope configurations for the 'that' phrase and negation, corresponding to the following:

(17a) $[\text{THAT}_{=b, Jwt} \ F^*: x] \ [\text{Not} \ [x \text{ is } G^*]]$

(17b) $\text{Not} \ [[\text{THAT}_{=b, Jwt} \ F^*: x] \ [x \text{ is } G^*]]$,

where $\text{THAT}_{=b, Jwt}$ is the four-place relation expressed by 'that' with the property of being identical to b and the property of being jointly instantiated in w, t (Jwt) saturating the second and third argument places, respectively.

(17a) and (17b) have importantly different truth conditions. (17a) is true at w' iff being identical to b and F^* are uniquely jointly instantiated in w,t in an object x and x is not G^* in w'. (17b) is true at w' iff the following is not the case: being identical to b and F^* are uniquely jointly instantiated in w,t in an object x and x is G^* in w'. Thus if (17a) is true at w', so is (17b). But (17b) could be true at w' without (17a) being true there. In particular, if b is in the domain of w' and fails to have F^* in w,t, (17b) is true at w' and (17a) isn't. And if b simply fails to exist at w', even if it is identical to b and has F^* in w,t, (17b) is true at w' and (17a) isn't.[15]

Sentences of the form (17) uttered in w,t by a speaker whose perceptual intention has as its object b usually have readings corresponding to (17a). Thus suppose I am at a party at Lake Tahoe in w,t and pointing at a man, b, across the room I say:

(18)   That man is not from California.

The truth of my utterance (in w,t—the context of utterance) would seem to require at least that b not be from California (and it seems to me to require that b be a man as well). It really does not seem as though b's not being a man (in w,t) by itself would *suffice* for the truth of my utterance (in w,t). But this would suffice for its truth, if it were read as (17b). The reading corresponding to (17a), by contrast, requires that in w,t, b is a man and is not from California. Thus, (18) uttered in the situation as described surely seems to be most naturally read as (17a).

When we consider similar examples, they all seem to have only the reading corresponding to (17a). As was the case with examples of the same form containing NDNS uses of 'that' phrases, this may well lead us to wonder whether sentences of the form (17) with the 'that' phrase used with a perceptual intention *ever* have the reading corresponding to (17b). And indeed, I think such readings are extremely difficult, though not impossible, to get. Why are such readings so suppressed?

In the first case, there is the general fact, noted earlier in connection with NDNS uses, that it is exceedingly difficult to get negation to take wide scope over *any* quantifier in a similar construction. Thus, again, it is hard to read *any* of the following with negation taking wide scope over the quantifier:

The present King of France is not bald.

Some student is not bald.

Every student is not bald.

Most students are not bald.

But I think there is another mechanism at work in examples like (18) that makes the wide scope negation reading even harder to get. In such examples, by hypothesis the speaker has a perceptual intention whose object is b. So the speaker intends to say something about b. The speaker also wants her audience to recognize that she intends to say something about b. So in the general case, the speaker will choose predicative material to combine with 'that' in forming her 'that' phrase that she believes b to satisfy, and that she believes her audience will recognize b to satisfy. In this way, she can get her audience to recognize the object of her intention and to understand her. But if her utterance of (17) is understood as (17b), that b isn't F^* in the context of her utterance suffices for its truth in that context. But this is in tension with her using the predicate that expresses F^* (i.e., 'F') to get her audience to recognize the object of her intention b. Thus in general she will not want to be taken as expressing (17b), and her audience generally won't interpret her this way. So intending to express (17b) when uttering (17) in a situation of the sort being considered undermines the role played by the predicate '*F*' in such cases. Similarly for interpreting one who utters (17) as intending to express (17b). This, in conjunction with the first point, *very strongly* suppresses the reading (17b) for (17).[16] All this suggests that readings corresponding to (17b) will be exceedingly hard to get and will only be present in quite unusual cases. And I believe this prediction is borne out. I provide four different cases.

Suppose I am giving some people a tour of my new very sophisticated special effects studio (in w,t). In the doorway ahead of us is an incredibly realistic holographic projection of a man.[17] I tell my amazed audience they are looking at a hologram with computer-generated features, and then add, pointing at the hologram:

(19)   So that man doesn't exist.

(19) seems true in this circumstance (the context of utterance). Further, I think my intention has an object in this case. It is the hologram, b. After all, it is b that I intend to talk about! But the true reading can't be the reading given by (17a). For the truth of that reading requires b to be a man in w,t *and* requires b not to exist in w,t. But *neither* of these things is the case.

By contrast, the reading of (19) corresponding to (17b) is as follows:

(19b)   Not [[THAT$_{=b, Jwt}$ man: x] [x exists]]

This, of course, is *true* in w,t, because being identical to b and being a man have no unique common instance there. Thus, it is quite plausible that the true reading of (19) in the circumstance is (19b). The reason the highly suppressed reading is allowed to emerge here is that, as noted above, the only other reading available apparently could not be true in w,t (the context of utterance).[18]

A related but slightly different case is one in which Alan has gone to a flea market and purchased for a shockingly low price what he was told is a diamond. He triumphantly shows several of us his prize. Greg, having examined the stone and having some knowledge of stones and gems, says:

(20)   That diamond isn't real.

Assuming Alan has been taken, Greg's remark seems true. But the true reading can't correspond to

(20a) $[[\text{THAT}_{=b,\,\text{J}wt} \text{ diamond: } x] \text{ Not } [x \text{ is real}]]$,

where b is the stone Alan bought and w,t the world and time of the context of utterance. For (20a)'s truth (in w,t) requires b to be a diamond (in w,t). Thus the true reading of Greg's remark must correspond to:

(20b) $\text{Not } [[\text{THAT}_{=b,\,\text{J}wt} \text{ diamond: } x] [x \text{ is real}]]$

That b is not a diamond suffices for the truth of (20b). Here again, presumably this reading comes through because (20a), the only remaining reading, is so odd. Indeed, it isn't clear what it would be for this reading to be true in w,t, requiring as it does that b be both a diamond and not real in w,t.

We turn finally to somewhat different examples. Suppose we have heard rumors of hauntings and spirits in a house in a certain town. Skeptical, we go there to see what is going on. When we arrive we are told by locals that, for our own protection, we may only view the area from a considerable distance. We get into position and we see what we are told is a great boulder that appears to be hovering in the air unsupported by anything. Skeptic that I am, I conclude that it cannot be a boulder hovering in the air without support, but I don't yet know how they are pulling off the trick. As I reflect on the situation, I wonder aloud to my friend whether it could be a hot air balloon painted like a boulder, or perhaps a holographic projection of a boulder. Or might it really be a boulder that is being supported in a way I can't see? I tell my friend that I am not quite sure how the trick is being performed, and pointing in the direction of the thing I say:

(21)   In any case, one thing is absolutely clear: that boulder is not hovering unsupported in the air.

Presumably, I don't intend to assert the reading of (21) given by:

(21a)   [THAT$_{=b, Jwt}$ boulder: x] [Not [x is hovering unsupported in the air]]

(where b is the object of my intention and w,t the world and time of the context of my utterance). For I don't wish to commit myself to the object of my intention being a boulder. Nor, does it seem, will I be taken this way. If what I am observing is a trick of any sort (it is a balloon; or a holographic projection; or it a boulder with hidden support; or ...), it seems to me my remark will have been true. But then it appears that the sentence in this situation is read as:

(21b)   Not [[THAT$_{=b, Jwt}$ boulder: x] [x is hovering unsupported in the air]]

So here again, it appears that negation takes wide scope over the 'that' phrase.[19]

Let us consider one final case. We are in an underwater vessel observing a pod of dolphins swimming and playing. I notice something odd. I realize that among the dolphins is a cleverly disguised miniature submarine. My colleagues have not yet realized this. Pointing at the small submarine, call it b, I say:

(22)   That dolphin is not part of the pod.

When my friends ask me how I know that, I tell them that the thing I pointed at is not a dolphin at all, but a miniature submarine. Again, my utterance of (22) seems true. And again, we have a scope ambiguity. The two readings of (22) can be represented as follows:

(22a) [THAT$_{=b,\,Jwt}$ dolphin: x] [Not [x is part of the pod]]

(22a) Not [[THAT$_{=b,\,Jwt}$ dolphin: x] [x is part of the pod]]

(where w,t are the world and time of the context of my utterance). Since b is not a dolphin, (22a) is false when evaluated in the context of my utterance. Thus (22) apparently is not read as (22a). By contrast (22b) is true when evaluated in the context of my utterance. Thus, the fact that (22) seems true in the situation as described suggests that it has the reading (22b) here, and that its 'that' phrase takes narrow scope with respect to negation.

To summarize, when we look at the data involving the interaction of 'that' phrases and negation, there is nothing that suggests 'that' phrases are not quantificational and much to suggest that they are. We find that we do get narrow scope readings for various uses of 'that' phrases relative to negation. And in cases where such readings are hard to get, *either* 'that' phrases behave like other quantifiers *or* there are additional features of 'that' phrases that strongly suppress the readings in question.

Next, we turn to the interaction of 'that' phrases and verbs of propositional attitude. Since our concern is primarily to show that 'that' phrases in their various uses can take narrow scope with respect to verbs of propositional attitude, we can be fairly brief.[20] In the first place, it should be clear that when sentences containing QI uses of 'that' phrases are embedded with respect to verbs of propositional attitude, the 'that' phrases can take narrow scope with respect to the verbs in question.[21] For example, the most natural reading of

(23) Cini believes that most avid skiers remember that first black diamond run they attempted to ski

is the reading on which a general belief is attributed to Cini, so that *both* quantifiers in the embedded sentence take narrow scope with respect to 'Cini believes'.

Similarly, it is easy to get such readings in the case of NDNS uses. Recall Scott, who had great appreciation for the hominid who discovered how to start fires. A colleague of Scott's, who knows Scott's views on the matter, says:

(24) Scott believes that that hominid who discovered how to start fires was a genius.

The ascription seems true. Yet Scott has only general beliefs and does not believe a singular proposition containing the brilliant hominid as a constituent.[22] So here again, the 'that' phrase must take narrow scope with respect to 'Scott believes'.

Finally, let us turn to the most interesting cases: those in which 'that' phrases are used with perceptual intentions. Suppose we are at a party at which evil and vindictive Alan has just been named CEO of the Chanticleer toy company. Some of the guests are aware of this and some are not. Sherry, a Chanticleer executive, has long believed that Alan despises her. She has just heard the bad news about his being named CEO. Sherry believes that as CEO, Alan will make her life miserable. She is moping around saying she must quit her job. Someone asks me what is wrong with Sherry. Pointing at Alan, I say:

(25) Sherry believes that guy who was just named CEO of Chanticleer hates her.

Again, of course, we have a scope ambiguity. The two propositions (25) is capable of expressing as uttered in that context are:

(25a) [[THAT$_{=b, Jwt}$ guy who was just named CEO of Chanticleer: x] [Sherry believes [x hates her]]]

(25b) Sherry believes [[THAT$_{=b, Jwt}$ guy who was just named CEO of Chanticleer: x] [x hates her]]

(where b is the object of my intention, Alan, and w,t the world and time of my context of utterance). The truth of (25a) in the context of utterance (w,t) requires there to be a unique instance x of being identical to b and being a guy who was just named CEO of Chanticleer in w,t, and requires Sherry to believe of x that he hates her. Put another way, the truth of (25a) requires b to be a guy who was just named CEO of Chanticleer and requires Sherry to believe the singular proposition that b hates her. But it does not require Sherry to believe that b is a guy who was just named CEO of Chanticleer. It seems to me that (25) is not read as (25a) in the present case. For I think we have the intuition that my utterance of (25) *explains* Sherry's behavior. But if (25) is read as (25a), it wouldn't explain her behavior. For it only ascribes to Sherry the belief that Alan hates her. But Sherry has believed *that* for some time, and that she has *this* belief does not explain her behavior. Intuitively, I have explained Sherry's behavior because part of the content of the belief I ascribe to her is that Alan was just named CEO. (25a) fails to capture this.

(25b)'s truth in w,t (the context of utterance), by contrast, requires Sherry to believe that something x is a unique common instance in w,t of being identical to b (Alan) and being a guy who was just named CEO of Chanticleer, and that x hates her. So for (25b) to be true in w,t, Sherry does have to believe in w,t that something is identical to Alan and is a guy who was just named CEO of

Chanticleer. Thus, (25) seems to favor the reading corresponding to (25b) in the situation as described. If (25) is read in this way, then it does, as it seems to, explain Sherry's foul mood.

That (25) does explain Sherry's behavior is supported by the fact that it seems true in the situation as described. For it to seem true, it must be a correct explanation of Sherry's behavior, and not merely be a true ascription of belief. As a response to the question as to why Sherry is behaving in a certain way, even a true, but not explanatorily relevant, belief ascription will seem (and be?) false. Thus suppose that when asked what is wrong with Sherry instead of (25) I say:

(26)   Sherry believes that Chanticleer is exploiting its workers.

If, as we are supposing, this does not explain Sherry's moping about, even if it ascribes to Sherry a belief she really has, it will seem false. Thus the fact that (25) seems true suggests that we do take it to be a proper explanation. And this, as already indicated, would seem to require reading it in such a way that it ascribes to Sherry a belief whose content includes that Alan was named CEO of Chanticleer. But then it seems it must be read as (25b).

Finally, I would add that if instead of (25) I had said

(27)   Sherry believes that Alan hates her.

or

(27′)   Sherry believes he [pointing at Alan] hates her.

there certainly is a feeling that I have not fully explained Sherry's behavior. Remember, she came to the party cheery, already believing that Alan hates her. Certainly, someone who knew this would be puzzled at (27)/(27′) as an attempt to explain Sherry's moping. What is missing, of course, is the ascription to Sherry of the belief that Alan was just named CEO. In the case of (25), however, we feel that Sherry's behavior is fully explained. This contrast between (25) and (27)/(27′) strongly suggests that (25) does in part ascribe to Sherry the belief that Alan was named Chanticleer CEO and thus is read as (25b) in the situation as described.

I believe that intuitions about the *falsity* of belief ascriptions in certain cases also provide evidence that 'that' phrases used with perceptual intentions can take narrow scope relative to verbs of propositional attitude. Suppose my friend Deena has her heart set on buying a diamond. She wants to get a good deal and has been dealing with Alan, a pretty shady character. Alan has shown her a large stone that she likes, but she wonders whether it is genuine. She asks her friend Ed to look at the stone and to tell her whether it is a diamond and whether it is valuable. Ed looks at the stone and he doesn't believe it is a diamond. However, for reasons that are not clear, Ed believes that the stone at one time belonged to Elvis Presley, and so he comes to the conclusion that the stone is valuable as a bit of Elvis memorabilia. Ed expresses this to Liz, Deena's acquaintance, as they both gaze at the stone, saying 'It isn't a diamond; but it is valuable'. It turns out the stone *is* a diamond, but it has little value (Ed was wrong on both counts: Elvis never owned it). Deena takes Liz to look at the stone again, and as they look at the stone says to Liz, "By the way, what did Ed say about the stone?" Liz nods at the stone and says:

(28)   Ed said that diamond is very valuable.

Intuitively, the ascription seems false in this case. The two readings that (28) has on the present view are:

(28a)   Ed said [[THAT$_{=b, Jwt}$ diamond: x] [x is valuable]]

(28b)   [[THAT$_{=b, Jwt}$ diamond: x] Ed said [x is valuable]] (where $\text{THAT}_{=b,Jwt}$ is the result of saturating the second and third argument places in the four-place relation expressed by 'that' with the properties of being identical to b, where b is the stone, and being jointly instantiated in w,t, where w and t are the world and time of the context of utterance, respectively). (28b) is true in the situation as described, since Ed did say of what is in fact a diamond that it is valuable. (28a) is false in the situation as described, since Ed did not say of the stone that it is a diamond (quite the contrary). Thus our intuition that the ascription is false in such a case suggests that (28) has the reading (28a) in this case. Further, our intuition that (28) is false in the case as described is traceable to the fact that in uttering (28) Liz appears to claim that Ed said that the stone is a diamond. And, of course, (28a) *is* false because it asserts that Ed said of the stone that it is a diamond. This again suggests that our intuition of falsity here is the result of (28)'s having the reading (28a).

Finally, note that if Liz had said:

(29)   Ed said that it is valuable

there would be little tendency to feel as though she spoke falsely: Ed did say of the stone that it is valuable. The difference in our intuitive reactions to (28) and (29) is best explained by holding that (28) is read as (28a) and so, unlike (29), entails that Ed said of the stone that it is a diamond (which, of course, he didn't).

All the various considerations raised here suggest that (28) does have the reading (28a) in this case. So again, we have good evidence that 'that' phrases used with perceptual intentions take narrow scope with respect to verbs of propositional attitude.

There is a final sort of case that provides evidence for the claim that 'that' phrases used with perceptual intentions take narrow scope with respect to verbs of propositional attitude. Suppose we are at a bar and there are a bunch of male transvestites there. It is obvious to all of us except Donnie, who is somewhat slow, that the people in question are men. Donnie, pointing at Alan, one of the transvestites, says 'That woman is beautiful'. Someone asks me what Donnie said. I say, pointing at Alan:

(30)   Donnie said that that woman is beautiful.

Intuitively, I have spoken truly here. Now as before, (30) should have a scope ambiguity. The two readings of (30) can be represented as follows:

(30a)   Donnie said [[THAT$_{=a, Jwt}$ woman: x] [x is beautiful]]

(30b)   [[THAT$_{=a, Jwt}$ woman: x] [Donnie said [x is beautiful]]]

(where THAT$_{=a, Jwt}$ is the result of saturating the second and third argument places in the four-place relation expressed by 'that' with the properties of being identical to Alan and being jointly instantiated in w,t, respectively where w,t, are the world and time of the context of utterance). Of course (30b) is false in the situation as described. For its truth requires Alan to be a woman in w,t (the world and time of the context of utterance). And he is not. By contrast, (30a) is true in the situation as described, since it seems plausible to suppose that Donnie said that Alan is a woman and is beautiful. But then since (30) seems true, it must have the reading (30a) here. It is worth adding that standard direct reference accounts, according to which for 'That F' to refer to b in a context, b must satisfy 'F' in that context, cannot hold that (30) is true in the situation as described. For since Alan is not a woman, 'That woman' cannot refer to him in the context of utterance. On such an account, 'That woman' in (30) apparently has no referent and so (30) cannot be true. Thus standard direct reference accounts cannot explain the truth of (30) in the situation as described. So here again, we have evidence that 'that' phrases used with perceptual intentions take narrow scope with respect to verbs of propositional attitude.[23]

Thus, more generally, I conclude that 'that' phrases *in their various uses* do take narrow scope relative to verbs of propositional attitude, as the present theory predicts.

Having considered the interaction of various uses of 'that' phrases with modal operators, negation, monotone decreasing quantifiers, and verbs of propositional attitude, it is worth briefly summarizing our discussion. As stated at the outset, we are particularly concerned with the question of whether there are narrow scope readings of 'that' phrases with respect to these various scoped elements. We have seen that 'that' phrases used in the various ways discussed *do* take narrow scope with respect to these other scoped elements and so exhibit the sort of behavior that we find exhibited by other quantifiers. Thus the data we have considered here strongly suggest that 'that' phrases are quantificational, just as the present theory claims.

This and That: A Variety of Loose Ends

Several issues remain to be discussed that don't fit neatly with the issues raised in previous chapters. Thus the present chapter comprises a collection of issues and loose ends that are bound together primarily in sharing this feature. However, they are all sufficiently important that they merit attention.

First, there is the matter of the possibility of perceptual intentions lacking objects in some situations. Most direct reference theorists allow that under certain extreme circumstances, no object is determined by the character of a 'that' phrase. These aren't merely cases where the demonstrated or intended object fails to satisfy the predicative material in the 'that' phrase; the failure is more dramatic. They are cases in which *nothing can be identified* as the demonstrated or intended object to begin with. Theorists may disagree about the circumstances under which this occurs, but so far as I can see, most theorists wish to allow for it. Perhaps all would agree that this occurs in the following case.[1] Suppose I am hallucinating that a new Porsche Boxster is sitting in front of me with the keys in it. Pleased with my apparent good luck, I "say of the car that isn't there":

(1)   That car is beautiful.

Many direct reference theorists believe that in such a case my 'that' phrase has no referent. Thus, I have not expressed a proposition at all, and so the sentence I utter is neither true nor false. Further, many think this is *intuitively* correct. *Intuitively*, they say, I didn't say anything true or false.

I simply wish to point out that the present theory seems to have this consequence as well. In such a case, I think I am perceiving something and I intend to make an assertion about the thing I take myself to be perceiving. But I am not in fact perceiving any such thing. Thus, I have a perceptual intention that has no object. In the case of a perceptual intention *with* an object, say b, my intending to talk about b determines the property of *being identical to b*, which then saturates the second argument place in the four-place relation expressed by 'that'. If there is no object of my intention, however, clearly my intention cannot determine the property of being identical to b, for b, the object of my intention. There is no such b! Thus, it seems plausible to hold in such a case that the intention in question determines no property at all. But then there is no property to saturate the second argument place in the four-place relation expressed by 'that'. This means that the relation contributed by 'that' to the "proposition" in such a case has a gap (i.e., an unsaturated argument place) in it where it shouldn't have a gap. And in turn, it is plausible to suppose that this means that the "proposition" is not truth evaluable, and so is not a proposition at all. In other words, just like on a direct reference theory, on the present view in such a case I will not have expressed a proposition and so will not have said something true or false.

Thus to the extent that people have found it intuitively plausible that in cases like the one described (or similar cases) nothing true or false is said by an utterance of (1), the present theory is able to accommodate this intuition.

This is a perhaps unexpected, and I think desirable, feature of a quantificational account of 'that' phrases.

The second loose end concerns properties possessed by determiners. To begin with, there is a property allegedly had by all determiners in all languages, usually referred to as *conservativeness*, that has been much discussed in the generalized quantifier literature. On the present account, though 'that', like other determiners, contributes to propositions a two-place relation between properties, it is importantly different from other, more typical determiners. First, it is contextually sensitive and contributes different relations to propositions on different occasions of use. Further, in the case of 'that' phrases used with perceptual intentions, the two-place relation between properties contributed is rather unusual and complex, involving as it does the properties of being identical to b (where b is the object of the perceptual intention) and being jointly instantiated in w,t (where w,t are the world and time of the context of utterance). This might raise the worry that on the present account 'that' will be fail to be conservative. This would be a very unwelcome result, since it would force advocates of the present view to hold that the determiner 'that' is a singular exception to what otherwise seems to be a universal semantic constraint on determiners.

The initial difficulty in addressing this problem is that it isn't clear what it means to be conservative in the context of the present theory. The usual definition assumes that determiners combine with terms denoting sets of individuals, and that determiners themselves denote relations between sets of individuals or functions from sets of individuals to sets of sets of individuals. Thus, for example, 'some' denotes the function that maps a set of individuals A to the set of all sets B such that A intersection B is nonempty; 'every' denotes the function that maps a set A to the sets of all sets B such that A is a subset of B; and so on. Within this framework, letting A,B be sets and D a determiner denotation (e.g., a function from sets to sets of sets), we can say that

D is conservative iff $B \in D(A)$ iff $A \cap B \in D(A)$

One can test determiners for this property by asking whether sentences like the following must be true, where F and G are arbitrary set terms and d is a determiner:

dF is G iff dF is GF

Thus, sentences like 'every man is happy iff every man is a happy man' and 'some man is happy iff some man is a happy man' show that 'every' and 'some' are conservative.

However, this notion of conservativeness cannot be applied directly to the present view. For we have determiners expressing relations between properties rather than sets. Worse yet, we have possible worlds and a distinction between the context of utterance of a sentence and the circumstance or world at which we evaluate the proposition expressed by a sentence in a context. Our denotation for 'that' needs to be saturated in a context with two properties to get a determiner denotation. And even then, we get a relation between properties that (in some cases) requires us to look at property instances in worlds that are not worlds in which the proposition expressed by the sentence containing 'that' is being evaluated. It just isn't obvious how to extend the usual definition so that it applies to such a thing.

In fact, it seems to me there are (at least) two notions that both seem to be natural extensions of the usual notion of conservativeness. Where d is a determiner and A and B are predicates expressing properties, we have the following condition, which I call *conservativeness in a context* (CIC):

(CIC) The proposition expressed in w,t by 'd A is B' is true in w,t iff the proposition expressed in w,t by 'd A is BA' is true in w,t.

The crucial point here is that the propositions expressed by the sentences in a context are then evaluated for truth *at the world and time of that very context* (I ignore all other elements of a context—e.g., the agent—except the world and time in this discussion). On the other hand, we have what I call *conservativeness across circumstances* (CAC):

(CAC) The proposition expressed in w,t by 'd A is B' is true in a circumstance w',t' iff the proposition expressed in w,t by 'd A is BA' is true in w',t'.

Here we allow the context of utterance and the circumstance of evaluation to be distinct.

Of course for typical quantifiers formed from determiners like 'some', 'every', 'most' and so on, these two notions converge. 'That' qua determiner, however, satisfies CIC but not CAC.[2] Is there any reason to think that this is a problem? I don't think so. We can still claim that all determiners satisfy CIC, and so we still have a very significant "semantic universal." Of course it might turn out that there is some deep explanation of why determiners are conservative, and that this explanation would require determiners to satisfy CAC. If this were to be the case, the present account would have a problem. But there is absolutely no reason to think that a deep explanation of why determiners are conservative *would* require this. And given that in simple, ordinary uses of quantifiers of the sort that fill our day to day lives we are concerned with evaluating the propositions expressed by sentences containing them at the worlds and times of the contexts of utterance of the sentences, there is every reason to think that any deep explanation of why determiners are conservative would only require determiners to satisfy CIC.

As the discussion of conservativeness may suggest, in the literature on generalized quantifiers in natural language much attention is devoted to which properties are possessed by which determiners. Since I have raised the issue of whether 'that' qua determiner is conservative, it is worth saying a bit more about the properties of 'that' or, more accurately, about the properties of the relations it contributes to propositions on certain uses. Consider a use of a 'that' phrase in a world and time w,t by a speaker who has a perceptual intention whose object is b. The speaker, let us suppose, utters 'That A is B' (here and henceforth in this discussion, I assume that 'A' and 'B' contain no indexicals, or other contextually sensitive expressions) and thereby expresses the following proposition:

(2) $[[\text{THAT}_{=b, Jwt} \; A^*: x] \; [B^*x]]$,

where A^* and B^* are the properties expressed by 'A' and 'B' respectively. $\text{THAT}_{=b, Jwt}$, of course, is the two-place relation between properties contributed to the proposition by 'that' as used in the context in question (__ and $=b$ are uniquely jointly instantiated in w,t in an object x and x is __). For (2) to be true at a world w', the properties A^* and B^* must stand in this relation at w'. But whether they do or not depends completely on the properties of b in w and w'. In particular, if b in w has A^* and in w' has B^*, the properties A^* and B^* stand in the relation in question and the proposition is true; otherwise, it is false. Thus, in the utterance of 'That A is B' that expressed (2), the determiner 'that' contributed to (2) a two-place relation between properties that obtains between the properties A^* and B^* at a world w' iff the particular individual b possesses A^* at w and B^* at w'. To repeat, in such a case, whether the relation 'that' contributes to a proposition obtains between properties, and hence whether the proposition containing the relation and those properties (in a given order) is true, depends on the properties possessed by a *particular individual*, b, at various worlds.

Many other determiners work very differently. Whether the proposition expressed by 'Every A is B' is true at a world w', that is, whether A^* and B^* stand in the relation expressed by 'every' there, depends only on how many things have A^* and not B^* at w. Its truth doesn't in any way depend on whether a *particular thing* b has A^* or B^* at w' or some other world.[3]

This can be made somewhat more precise as follows. Let D be the domain of individuals of world w'. Let f be a one-one function from D onto D. Finally, for an n-place relation R ($n > 0$—for $n = 1$, R is a property), if the extension of R at w' is $S \leq D^n$, let $f(S) = \{\langle f(o_1), \ldots, f(o_n) \rangle \mid \langle o_1, \ldots, o_n \rangle \in S\}$. Now let world w'' be the *f-permutation of w'* iff D is the domain of w'', and for an n-place relation R, the extension of R at $w'' = f(S)$, where S is the extension of R at w'. If the proposition expressed by 'Every A is B' is true at w', it is true at the f-permutation of w', for arbitrary f (and vice versa). For suppose 'Every A is B' is true at w'. Then every element of D (the domain of w') that has A^* (the property expressed by 'A') in w' has B^* (the property expressed by 'B') in w'. Now consider an f-permutation w'' of w'. The extension of A^* at $w'' = \{f(o) \mid o \in$ extension of A^* at $w'\}$; and the extension of B^* at $w'' = \{f(o) \mid o \in$ extension of B^* at $w'\}$. So consider an arbitrary thing a in the extension of A^* at w''. Then a $= f(o)$ for some o in the extension of A^* at w'. But o is in the extension of B^* at w' (everything that has A^* has B^* in w'). But then $f(o)$ is in the extension of B^* at w''. That is, a is in the extension of B^* at w''. Thus everything that has A^* at w'' has B^* at w''. So 'Every A is B' is true at w''.

But (2) could be true at w' and false at an f-permutation of it. Since the truth of (2) at a world requires b to have B^*

there, we need only suppose that b is in the extension of B^* at w' and not at w'' (thus we need only suppose that f does not map any element of the extension of B^* at w' to b).

Loosely following the literature, let us call determiners such that when they occur in sentences those sentences express propositions whose truth values don't shift across f-permutations of a given world for arbitrary f, *logical*.[4] Thus the above considerations show that 'every' is logical and 'that' isn't.

Though there are *syntactically complex* nonlogical determiners (e.g., 'every __ but John'—see below), it may be that all *syntactically simple* determiners other than 'that', assuming we are correct about how it works, are logical.[5] Thus, my view may require us to say that 'that' violates an otherwise universal semantic constraint on *syntactically simple* determiners.

And indeed, I have only used logicality as an example here (and this is why my discussion has been somewhat loose). We began by worrying that, because of the unusual semantic properties the present view attributes to the determiner 'that', it may fail to possess a property, conservativeness, that is apparently possessed by all determiners in all human languages. We responded by showing that on the view of 'that' we have adopted, it does satisfy (one way of extending the notion of) conservativeness. However, the new worry we have raised is whether the present view of 'that' might result in a violation of an otherwise universal semantic constraint on *syntactically simple* determiners. The case of (some notion of) logicality was intended to provide a possible, illustrative example.

I am inclined to think that my view of 'that' may indeed result in attributing properties to it that result in its being an exception to some constraint that all other syntactically simple determiners satisfy, whether the constraint concerns some notion of logicality or some other property. This is because, as I have said from the outset, on the present view 'that' works in ways that are importantly different from the way other determiners work. In particular, allowing a "double supplementation" by properties determined by the intentions of the speaker is something that no other determiner does. Having this feature means that 'that' allows these properties determined by the intentions of the speaker to be "built into" the two-place relation between properties it contributes to propositions.

But this in turn should lead us to *expect* that 'that' may behave more like a syntactically complex determiner than a syntactically simple one in certain respects. For consider a syntactically complex *nonlogical* determiner like 'every __ but John' (which occurs in sentences like 'Every student but John was present'). The nonlogicality of the determiner results from a *lexical item* in the complex determiner (e.g., 'John') making a contribution to the two-place relation contributed to propositions by the determiner. In the case of 'that', speaker intentions, rather than lexical items, play this role by determining properties (e.g., *is identical to John*) that figure in the two-place relation that is contributed to propositions. But then the only difference in the two cases is which *vehicle*, speaker intentions or lexical items, makes the contribution that results in nonlogicality to the two-place relation between properties that is then contributed to the proposition. Hence, it would not at all be surprising if 'that' in such respects semantically behaved more like a syntactically complex determiner than a simple one. Indeed, given the way I claim 'that' works and what I have just said, this is surely to be expected! So that 'that' fails to be logical, as do some syntactically complex determiners such as 'every __ but John', or that, more generally, it fails to satisfy some constraint satisfied by all other syntactically simple determiners is neither surprising nor problematic. Such constraints can be reconstrued as constraints on syntactically simple determiners that don't allow the sort of supplementation allowed by 'that'; and we can give a principled explanation why we would expect 'that' to behave in some respects more like certain syntactically complex determiners. To repeat, the idea is that speaker intentions contribute to the propositional contribution of 'that' as used in a context in the way that lexical items contribute to the propositional contribution of a syntactically complex determiner. So, again, it is hardly surprising that 'that' semantically behaves in some respects like a syntactically complex determiner.

The third loose end to be tied up concerns the relation between the phenomenon of the semantics of 'that' allowing for supplementation by speakers' intentions and the phenomenon of so-called *quantifier domain restriction*.[6] Beginning with the latter, it is well known that in uttering sentences containing quantifiers such as

(3)   Every student passed the exam,

I will often succeed in communicating to my audience a more restricted claim than appears to be expressed by the sentence I utter. In uttering (3), for example, I might succeed in communicating to my audience the claim that every student *in a particular class* passed the exam. Views as to how I succeed in communicating this latter claim differ. On some accounts, my utterance of (3) literally expresses (only) the proposition that every student (in the universe) passed the exam, and I manage to *convey* the proposition that every student in a particular class passed the exam by *pragmatic* means.[7] On other views, an utterance of (3) literally *semantically* expresses a proposition in which the quantification is more restricted than it might initially appear. On a view of this sort, an utterance of (3) may well *semantically* express the proposition that every student in a particular class passed the exam.[8]

Suppose a view of the latter sort is correct (I am not here *endorsing* such a view, but if such a view is not correct, the worry I go on to consider simply doesn't arise—see note 12 below). It might be thought that it is the speaker's intentions that somehow serve to further restrict the domain of quantification. But if this were so, it would give rise to the following worry. I have claimed that the semantics of 'that' allows for supplementation by speakers' intentions. One way in which this occurs is that properties determined by the speaker's intentions further restrict the quantification expressed by the 'that' phrase (this leaves out *being jointly instantiated* and *being jointly instantiated in w,t*—the other properties determined by speakers' intentions).[9] Further, I claim that this is a unique feature of 'that' phrases qua quantifiers. Other quantifiers do not have this feature as part of their semantics. And I have explained the contextual sensitivity of 'that' phrases and, for example, differences in the behavior of 'that' phrases and definite descriptions by reference to the fact that the semantics of 'that' allows for the sort of supplementation just described, whereas the semantics of other determiners, and 'the' in particular, does not. But if a semantic account of quantifier domain restriction according to which speakers' intentions in some way serve to further restrict the quantification that is *semantically* expressed by a quantifier phrase in an utterance of a sentence like (3) is correct, it appears that *all* quantifiers *semantically* allow supplementation by speakers' intentions. But then it appears that I could not appeal to the fact that the semantics of 'that' phrases allows for such supplementation and definite descriptions do not to explain differences in the behavior of the two types of expressions. Nor could I account for the contextual sensitivity of 'that' phrases, as a feature other quantifiers lack, by appeal to the fact that 'that' phrases are unique in allowing supplementation by speakers' intentions. Thus, assuming a semantic account of quantifier domain restriction according to which speakers' intentions serve to further restrict the quantification that is *semantically* expressed by an utterance of a sentence like (3), it is worth asking whether this phenomenon can be teased apart from the type of supplementation I claim the semantics of 'that' *uniquely* allows.

Given certain plausible assumptions, it appears that these things can be teased apart. In particular, I shall assume that the correct account of quantifier domain restriction holds that it is the semantic value of the N′ constituent of a quantifier phrase that is altered in further restricting the domain of quantification. It seems to me that the most plausible accounts of quantifier domain restriction (understood as a semantic phenomenon) do hold this.[10] This means that in the case of (3) as used in a particular context, somehow the N′ constituent 'student' gets assigned as its semantic value something more restricted than the set of students or the property of being a student. Theories may vary as to the mechanism by means of which this occurs. So, for example, one might hold, with Stanley and Szabo (2000), that nominals or N′ constituents have indices at the level of LF. These indices (when not bound by other quantifiers) get assigned values when the nominals or N′ constituents are used in a context, and the semantic value assigned to a nominal or N′ constituent is affected by what is assigned its index. So, for example, the index on 'student' when (3) is uttered in a particular context might get assigned the property of being in a given class with the result that the N′ 'student' in such a case has as its semantic value the property of being a student in this class. There are other ways of implementing the sort of view I am considering.[11] However the view is implemented, whether in the way just described or in some other way, we assume that quantifier domain restriction is handled by the N′

constituents in quantifier phrases being assigned different semantic values in different contexts.

We can now see at least in principle how the phenomenon of the semantics of 'that' allowing for supplementation by speaker intentions can be distinguished from the phenomenon of quantifier domain restriction as just described. For on the present view, it is the semantic value of the *determiner* 'that' that varies with speaker intentions. More specifically, the properties determined by a speaker's intentions in using the determiner 'that' affect which two-place relation between properties the determiner as used in that context contributes to the proposition expressed. By contrast, quantifier domain restriction, we are assuming, works by the semantic value of the N' *constituent* in a quantifier phrase varying with context. And these, of course, are quite different. Thus we are free to hold that the sort of supplementation we are claiming 'that' allows is unique to it (and things like it, such as 'this', 'those', etc.) and so does not occur with other determiners.[12]

And indeed, there is evidence that the two phenomena differ in just the way claimed. In particular, data involving N' anaphora and N' ellipsis provide strong support for the view that the two phenomena are distinct. Let us begin with N' anaphora. If an account of quantifier domain restriction of the sort we are considering is correct, then we would expect certain things to happen in cases of N' anaphora on N' constituents of quantifier phrases. In particular, suppose we are discussing a bunch of bottles of alcohol we have just purchased. So when 'bottles' occurs as an N' constituent in quantifiers in sentences we utter in this context, it has the semantic value of 'bottles we just bought'. Now someone asks me who has been drinking from the bottles. I say:

(4) John drank from every bottle and Sean drank from one too.

Given what we have just said, the quantification in the first conjunct is over bottles we just bought. On the most natural reading of (4), the anaphor 'one' in the second conjunct ranges over bottles we just bought as well. We should expect (4) to have this reading if quantifier domain restriction works in the way we have claimed. For an N′ anaphor like 'one' in (4) should have a reading on which it gets its semantic value from its antecedent 'bottles'.[13] And on the view of quantifier domain restriction we are assuming, the semantic value of 'bottles' in (4) as used in the context described is the property of being a bottle we just bought. Thus the anaphor is picking up the semantic value of its antecedent in this case, as we would expect it to be able to do. This perhaps provides some support for the sort of view of quantifier domain restriction we are (for the sake of argument) assuming is correct.

Returning to 'that' phrases, suppose that as before we are discussing some bottles of alcohol we just bought and someone asks me who has been drinking from the bottles. I say, pointing at a bottle:

(5)   John drank from that bottle and Sean drank from one too.

Call the bottle I pointed at b. On the view we have defended, being identical to b will saturate the second argument place in the four-place relation expressed by 'that', and in so doing it will serve to further restrict the quantification the 'that' phrase expresses. But because it does so by affecting the semantic value of the *determiner* 'that' (unlike what occurs in quantifier domain restriction), the semantic value of the N′ 'bottle' will not be affected. Thus, the semantic value of the N′ 'bottle' in the first conjunct of (5) ought to be the property of being one of the bottles we just bought, as it was before. 'One' in the second conjunct should have a reading on which it picks this up as its semantic value as well. But we should *not* expect 'one' to be able to pick up as its semantic value the property of being one of the bottles we bought that is identical to b. Since the property of being identical to b saturates an argument in the relation expressed by the *determiner* 'that', there is no reason that it should be able to affect the semantic value of an N' anaphor. Hence 'one' in (5) should have a reading on which it ranges over bottles we just bought and should not have a reading on which it ranges over *bottles we just bought that are identical to b*. But then (5) should have a reading on which it is made true by John drinking from one bottle in the collection in question and Sean drinking from another; and it should not have a reading that *requires* both John and Sean to have drunk from b. This is clearly correct! Hence (5) provides evidence that the process whereby 'that' is supplemented by speakers' intentions is a very different phenomenon from the process whereby quantifier domains are restricted.

To summarize, when speakers' intentions (or whatever) restrict the domain of quantification by affecting the semantic value of the N' constituent of the quantifier, a proform 'one' with the N' constituent as antecedent *may* pick up this semantic value, as occurs in (4). However, when speakers' intentions determine a property P and so affect the denotation of the determiner 'that', thereby restricting the domain over which the quantifier it occurs in ranges, a proform 'one' whose antecedent is the N' constituent of the 'that' phrase *cannot* have its semantic value affected by P, as (5) illustrates. This is strong evidence that the phenomenon of quantifier domain restriction and the phenomenon whereby speaker intentions supplement 'that' are quite different.

Consider now an NDNS case. A friend and I are at Scott's Great Moments in Hominid History Fair. We see a project about the hominid who discovered how to start fires. While looking at it in the distance, I ask my friend about the science projects some boys she knows are working on. She replies:

(6)   Oddly enough, Ken's project concerns that early hominid and Greg's project is about one too.

Presumably, her intentions determined the property of being an early hominid who discovered how to start fires. This property saturates the second argument place in the four-place relation expressed by 'that', so that the first conjunct of her utterance of (6) expresses the proposition that Ken's project concerns the unique instance of being an early hominid who discovered how to start fires. But again, because this saturation affects only the semantic value of the determiner 'that', and not the semantic value of the N′ constituent 'early hominid', we would expect the N′ constituent 'early hominid' to have as its semantic value the property of being an early hominid. Further, we would expect the N′ anaphor 'one' in the second conjunct to be able to pick up this same semantic value from its antecedent in the first conjunct. But we would *not* expect the N′ anaphor to be able to pick up as its semantic value the property of being an early hominid who discovered how to start fires (since the latter property saturates an argument place in the four-place relation expressed by the *determiner* 'that'). Thus, we would expect the second conjunct to have a reading on which its truth requires that Greg's project is about an early hominid; and *not* to have a reading on which its truth *requires* that Greg's project is about an early hominid who discovered how to start fires. Again, this is clearly correct. So again here we have evidence that the supplementation by speakers' intentions that occurs in the case of 'that' is distinct from the general phenomenon of quantifier domain restriction.

That the explanation of the readings had by (5) and (6) has to do with the fact that 'that', unlike other determiners, allows supplementation by speakers' intentions is powerfully supported by certain differences between the behavior of 'that' phrases and definite descriptions in similar cases. To see this, consider the following sentence, which is odd or infelicitous:

*(7)   John met the current president of the United States and Laslo met one too.

The oddity presumably results from the fact that 'one' here picks up the semantic value of its antecedent and so ranges over current presidents of the United States. But because 'one' occurs in the second conjunct instead of 'him', the second conjunct strongly suggests (or perhaps even entails) that there is more than one current president of the United States and that Laslo met a different president than John did. However, the use of 'the' in the first conjunct entails (or perhaps just suggests) that there is a unique current U.S. president. This conflict between the first and second conjuncts leads to oddness or infelicity.

Now consider the following case. We are looking at a sign with the name of a book, *Bubbles in Rongovia*, on it. Not knowing who the author of *Bubbles in Rongovia* is but assuming there is a unique author and clearly intending to say something about him or her, I say:

*(8)   Harold knows the author and Scott knows one too.

Again, the sentence is odd or infelicitous. Still assuming a semantic account of quantifier domain restriction of the sort we have been discussing, the reason is that the N' 'author' here has as its semantic value the property of being author of *Bubbles in Rongovia*. Thus 'one' in the second conjunct has a reading on which it picks up the semantic value of its antecedent and ranges over authors of *Bubbles in Rongovia*. But then the use of 'one' in the second conjunct implies or suggests that there is more than one author of *Bubbles in Rongovia*, whereas the use of 'the' in the first conjunct suggests or implies that there is a single author. Thus the two conjuncts conflict, just as they did in (7), and we again get oddness. Note that it is the fact that the semantic value of the first conjunct N′ 'author' has as its semantic value the property of being author of *Bubbles in Rongivia*, owing to the process of quantifier domain restriction, and that 'one' in the second conjunct picks up this semantic value, that gives rise to oddness here.

Suppose now that the case is just as before. Looking at the sign before us and not knowing who the author of *Bubbles in Rongovia* is, I form the descriptive intention to talk about the thing uniquely possessing the property of being the author of *Bubbles in Rongovia*, and so my intention determines this property. I then produce the following NDNS use of a 'that' phrase:

(9)   Harold knows that author and Scott knows one too.

Here the sentence is perfectly fine! And my account of the semantics of 'that' phrases explains why it is fine, unlike (8). Here my intentions determine a property that saturates the second argument place in the four-place relation expressed by 'that'. Thus the property has an effect on the semantic value of the *determiner* 'that', but has no effect on the semantic value of the N′ 'author'. So the semantic value of this N′ is the property of being an author. 'One' in the second conjunct picks up this value and so ranges over authors (not authors of *Bubbles in Rongovia*). So even though on our view the first conjunct of (9) entails that there is a unique author of *Bubbles in Rongovia*, there is no conflict between the first and second conjuncts, since the semantic value of the N′ anaphor in the second conjunct is the property of being an author. That (8) is odd or infelicitous and (9) isn't and that my account predicts exactly why this would occur provides powerful support to my theory and strongly suggests that the phenomenon of quantifier domain restriction and the phenomenon of 'that' allowing supplementation by speakers' intentions are distinct phenomena.

N' ellipsis data provide evidence to the same effect. Again, if an account of quantifier domain restriction of the sort under consideration is correct, we would expect certain things to occur in cases of N' ellipsis. Let us again suppose we are discussing a bunch of bottles of alcohol we have just purchased. So when 'bottles' occurs as an N' constituent in quantifiers in sentences we utter in this context, as before it has the semantic value of 'bottles we just bought'. Someone says

(10)   Most bottles are half empty and some are broken.

In the second conjunct we have an elided N' constituent 'bottles'. Here again, the elided N' constituent in the second conjunct is most naturally read as having the same semantic value as the N' constituent in the first conjunct. That is, if the first conjunct is "about" bottles we just bought (so that the semantic value of the N' constituent is the property of being a bottle we just bought), the second conjunct is naturally read as being "about" those same bottles (i.e., the elided N' constituent has the same semantic value as its antecedent).[14] Of course, we would expect an elided N' constituent to be able to pick up the semantic value of its antecedent.

Now consider what happens when 'that' phrases contain the antecedents in N' ellipsis. Suppose we are waiting for a bunch of climbers to return from a very strenuous climb. A friend walks up and asks me whether the climbers are done and if I know anything about their physical condition. Pointing at a climber, say b, who has just completed the climb, I say:

(11)   That climber is completely exhausted and some are still on the mountain.

On the present account of 'that' phrases, the property of being identical to b saturates the second argument place in the four-place relation expressed by 'that', thereby restricting the first conjunct's quantification to climbers identical to b. As before, because it is the propositional contribution of the *determiner* 'that' that is affected here, this has no effect on the semantic value of the N′ constituent in the first conjunct, which should be the property of being a climber. Hence we would expect the elided N′ constituent in the second conjunct to have a reading on which it picks up the semantic value of its antecedent. Thus, we would expect the second conjunct to have a reading on which the quantifier in it ranges over climbers. But, since the property of being identical to b saturates an argument place in the four-place relation expressed by the *determiner* 'that', we would not expect it to be capable of affecting the semantic value of the elided N′ constituent. Thus we would expect the second conjunct to have no reading on which the quantifier in it ranges over climbers who are identical to b, so that its truth *requires* some climbers who are identical to b to still be on the mountain. Again, this is clearly correct.

Turning finally to an NDNS case involving N′ ellipsis, suppose we are looking at the exhibit concerning the hominid who discovered how to start fires. My friend asks me about the intelligence of early hominids. Intending to talk about the hominid who discovered how to start fires, I say:

(12)   Obviously, that early hominid was smart, but some were not too bright.

Here my intentions determine the property of being a hominid who discovered how to start fires. This property saturates the second argument place in the four-place relation expressed by 'that', thereby restricting the quantification in the first conjunct to early hominids who discovered how to start fires. But again, this shouldn't affect the semantic value of the N′ constituent 'early hominid', which should have as its semantic value the property of being an early hominid. Thus, the elided material in the second conjunct should have a reading on which it picks up this semantic value, and on which the quantifier in the second conjunct ranges over early hominids. But the second conjunct should have no reading on which its truth requires that some early hominids who discovered how to start fires were not so bright. As before, our predictions are borne out.

To summarize the data to this point involving elided material ((10)–(12)), in cases like (10) in which "ordinary" quantifier domain restriction occurs, the elided N′ constituent in the second conjunct can be and is most naturally read as having the same semantic value as its first conjunct antecedent, whose semantic value has been "altered" by the context or the speaker's intentions ('bottles' in the first conjunct has as its semantic value the property of being a bottle we just bought). However, in cases in which the speaker's intentions determine a property P that supplements the semantic value of 'that' in the context ((11), (12)), thereby restricting the domain over which the quantifier it occurs in ranges, the elided material in the second conjunct cannot be read as having its semantic value affected by P.

As in the case of N′ anaphora, differences in the behavior of definite descriptions and 'that' phrases in cases of N′ ellipsis add powerful additional support to my account here. So, again, imagine that we are looking at a sign with the name of the book *Bubbles in Rongovia* on it. Not knowing who the author is, I say:

*(13)   Mark knows the author and Scott knows some too.

As before, we get infelicity or oddness. The reason is that in this case the N′ 'author' has as its semantic value the property of being an author of *Bubbles in Rongovia*. The ellided N′ in the second conjunct has a reading on which it picks up this semantic value, and so the whole sentence has a reading on which it asserts that Mark knows the author of *Bubbles in Rongovia* and Scott knows some author of *Bubbles of Rongovia*. Again, the implication of uniqueness in the first conjunct and the implication of nonuniqueness in the second conjunct combine to produce oddness or infelicity.[15]

Suppose now that the case is the same; looking at the sign before us and not knowing who the author of *Bubbles in Rongovia* is, I form the descriptive intention to talk about the thing uniquely possessing the property of being the author of *Bubbles in Rongovia*, and so my intention determines this property. I then produce the following NDNS use of a 'that' phrase:

(14)   Mark knows that author and Scott knows some too.

Again, the sentence is significantly better than the example with the definite description. And, of course, my account of the semantic of 'that' phrases explains why it is better. My intentions determine a property that saturates the second argument place in the four-place relation expressed by 'that'. Thus the property has an effect on the semantic value of the *determiner* 'that', but cannot affect the semantic value of the N′ 'author'. So the semantic value of this N′ is the property of being an author. The elided N′ in the second conjunct picks up this value and so ranges over authors (not authors of *Bubbles in Rongovia*). So even though on my view the first conjunct of (14) entails that there is a unique author of *Bubbles in Rongovia*, there is no conflict between the first and second conjuncts.[16] For on the reading in question, the second conjunct simply asserts that Scott knows some author (not some author of *Bubbles in Rongovia*).

Thus, it appears that the phenomenon of quantifier domain restriction and the phenomenon of the semantics of 'that' allowing for supplementation by speakers' intentions are quite different. The former results in N′ *constituents* having different semantic values in different contexts, and the latter results in the *determiner* 'that' having different semantic values (i.e., contributing different relations to propositions) in different contexts. As we have seen, data involving N′ anaphora and N′ ellipsis support this view. It is particularly striking that the present account of 'that' phrases explains and predicts differences in the behavior of definite descriptions and 'that' phrases. This constitutes powerful support for the account! Thus, the general phenomenon of quantifier domain restriction does not conflict with my claim that 'that' (and its ilk) are unique among determiners in allowing supplementation by speakers' intentions of the sort described.[17]

The fourth and final loose end concerns whether the semantic account I have sketched of 'that' *phrases* is to be extended to *syntactically simple* demonstratives such as 'that' (henceforth *simple 'that'*).[18] I don't intend to resolve this question here, since doing so would require going through data involving simple 'that' in the way we have for 'that' phrases and hence would effectively require a second monograph. However, I do wish to make some remarks on this topic.

The first question that arises here is whether any of the arguments I gave against a direct reference account of 'that' phrases work as arguments against a direct reference account of simple 'that'. We should expect that *some* of the arguments against direct reference accounts of 'that' phrases will not go through as arguments against direct reference accounts of simple 'that'. For example, we cannot form Bach-Peters sentences with simple 'that' for the simple reason that there is no relative clause to contain a pronoun that is anaphoric on another occurrence of simple 'that'. Thus we cannot use Bach-Peters sentences containing simple 'that' to argue against direct reference accounts of simple 'that'. On the other hand, we can test for weak crossover effects, and it *may* be that weak crossover data favor the view that simple 'that' is quantificational. Suppose I point at a house, saying:

(15)   Its pool is behind that.

It is hard to get a reading of (15) on which 'Its' is anaphoric on 'that' (so that (15) is true iff the house I indicate has a pool behind it). Of course, I don't mean to suggest that this is the last word on the weak crossover data. I am just pointing out that one *might* be able to marshal weak crossover data in favor of the view that simple 'that' is quantificational.

In any case, the general moral here is that if one wanted to argue that simple 'that' is quantificational, one ought to go through the arguments given against the direct reference account of 'that' phrases case by case. In each instance, one would either have to show that the argument worked against a direct reference account of simple 'that' as well, or explain why, given differences between simple 'that' and 'that' phrases that the quantificational theorist about simple 'that' is prepared to admit (e.g., lack of relative clauses in simple 'that'), one should not expect the argument to work.

Suppose one were able to show that some of the arguments against a direct reference account of 'that' phrases work for simple 'that' as well (and that, given differences between simple 'that' and 'that' phrases, we shouldn't expect the others to work). Obviously, this would provide motivation for asking whether we could extend the quantificational account of 'that' phrases to cover simple 'that' in a way that is empirically adequate to the behavior of simple 'that'. Or even suppose one were able to explain why *none* of the arguments against direct reference accounts of 'that' phrases carries over to simple 'that', given differences between the former and the latter that even a quantificational theorist about simple 'that' could admit. One might still then ask whether we could extend the quantificational account of 'that' phrases to handle simple 'that', and so have a unified account of 'that' as it occurs in 'that' phrases *and* on its own. How might such an extension of the present account go?

Well, first, how ought we think of the syntax? A natural idea is that a sentence that appears to be of the form

(16) $[_s[_{np}\text{That}]\ [_{vp}\text{is}\ F]]$

has an empty or covert (not phonologically or inscriptionally realized) N$'$ constituent in the NP containing 'that', and so has the following syntactical structure:

(16a) $[_s[_{np}[_{det}\text{That}]\ [_{n'}\text{e}]]\ [_{vp}\text{ is }F]]$,

where e is the empty N$'$ constituent.[19] There may be other ways to think of the syntax (e.g., we could even suppose there is an unfilled N$'$ position, rather than an N$'$ position filled by a empty constituent). For present purposes we shall stick with (16a), since we are simply trying to indicate how an extension of the quantificational account to simple 'that' *might* go.

If 'that' is to be univocal, when it occurs as simple 'that', it still must have as its lexical meaning the four-place relation __ *and* __ *are uniquely* __ *in an object x and x is* __. And one would presume that when speakers use simple 'that' in a context, the speaker's intentions would still determine properties (of the sort described earlier) that saturate the second and third argument places in this relation, with the result that simple 'that' as used in the context in question contributes to the proposition expressed by the sentence in which it occurs a two-place relation between properties. The crucial question is how to think of the contribution that the empty N' constituent e makes to propositions. If we suppose that someone who has a perceptual intention whose object is b utters in w,t an instance of (16)/(16a), she expresses the following proposition:

(16b) $[[[\text{THAT}_{=b,\text{J}wt}] [??]] [F^*]]$,

where $\text{THAT}_{=b,\text{J}wt}$ is the four-place relation expressed by 'that' with its second and third argument places saturated by *being identical to b* and *being jointly instantiated in w,t*, respectively; F^* is the property expressed by 'F'; and the question marks take the place of the propositional contribution of the empty N' constituent (here and henceforth I leave out variables in my representations of propositions).

It seems to me that there are at least three accounts we might give of this contribution. First, we might say that it is a property that is somehow determined by the context of utterance. Of course, something would have to be said about the mechanism whereby context determines the property expressed by our empty N' constituent. But if we suppose that in the context we are considering the property so determined is G^*, then in this context the utterance of (16)/(16a) expresses the following proposition:

(16c) $[[[\text{THAT}_{=b,\,Jwt}]\;[G^*]]\;[F^*]]$.

(16c) is true at an arbitrary world w' iff G^* and being identical to b are uniquely jointly instantiated in w,t in some object x and x is F^* at w'.

Second, we might think that the empty N' constituent always contributes to propositions some one and the same property that is always possessed by everything that exists, for example, the property T^* of *being a thing*. On this view, the empty N' constituent always contributes the same thing to a proposition and has no significant effect on its truth conditions, since the property it contributes is possessed by everything. On this view, (16)/(16a) in the context in question expresses the following proposition:

(16d) $[[[\text{THAT}_{=b,\,Jwt}]\;[T^*]]\;[F^*]]$,

which is true at an arbitrary world w' iff T^* and being identical to b are uniquely jointly instantiated (again, remember that everything that exists possess T^*) in w,t in some object x and x is F^* at w'.

Finally, we might suppose that the empty N' constituent contributes to propositions the property that is determined by the speaker's intentions in uttering 'that' and that fills the second argument place in the four-place relation expressed by 'that'. In this case, that property is *being identical to b*. On this view, the property of being identical to b gets into the proposition twice: once as a result of being determined by the speaker's intentions and so saturating an argument place in the four-place relation expressed by 'that'; and a second time since the empty N' constituent picks up as its semantic value (in that context) the property so determined.[20] In this case, the utterance of (16)/(16a) in the described situation expresses the following proposition:

(16e) $[[[\text{THAT}_{=b,\,Jwt}]\;[=b]]\;[F^*]]$,

which is true at an arbitrary world w' iff being identical to b and being identical to b are uniquely jointly instantiated in w,t in an object x and x is F^* at w' (iff b exists at w and is F^* at w').

Prior to a serious investigation of these tentative extensions of my account to simple 'that', I am inclined to favor this last option. For one thing, it might best explain why 'that' qua determiner can occur without an overt N$'$ constituent.[21] On my account, 'that' is unique among determiners in allowing for a property determined by the speaker's intentions to saturate an argument place in the relation it expresses and in so doing *restricting* the quantification to things that possess that property. In general, of course, the function of the N$'$ constituent combined with a determiner to form a quantifier is also to restrict the quantification to things possessing the property expressed by the N$'$ constituent.[22] But then if 'that' allows for a "built in" restriction, determined by the intentions of the speaker, one could see how in the limiting case it would semantically require no *further* restriction contributed by an N$'$ constituent. Thus, no *overt* N$'$ constituent is required, while, since no further restriction on the quantification is semantically required, the covert N$'$ constituent simply picks up the restriction already in place. Thus 'that' occurs comfortably without an overt N$'$ constituent.

A second advantage of this approach is that it neatly extends to allow for, oddly enough, (something like) QI uses of simple 'that' (as well as NDNS uses, which I won't discuss). There may by such uses, even though simple 'that' contains no *overt* N$'$ constituent containing a pronoun to be bound by a higher quantifier. For example, suppose we are watching a movie in which a woman wakes up on her first day of retirement. I say:

(17) Everybody looks forward to that.

From the context, it might be clear that I intended to convey the proposition that everybody looks forward to the unique first day of his or her retirement. In such a case, as discussed earlier, my intention determines the *relation*: *y is the first day of x's retirement* (henceforth Fyx). If (17) really is a QI use and my account is correct when applied to simple 'that' in the way under discussion, this means that Fyx saturates the second argument place in the four-place relation expressed by 'that' *and* is therefore also the semantic value of our null N' constituent (thus we would allow that such constituents can contribute to propositions *n*-place relations for arbitrary *n*). Thus, (17), again assuming it really contains a QI use and that my account extends to simple 'that', in the context in question expresses a proposition that is true iff for everybody x there is a unique instance y of being the first day of x's retirement and x looks forward to y. Again, I am not claiming that (17) *really is* a QI use. Such examples would have to be dissected carefully before coming to that conclusion. However, treating it along the lines discussed is interesting and suggestive.

In any case, these remarks are highly speculative. I simply want to give readers a sense of various ways in which the account might be extended to handle simple 'that' (and 'this'). Whether any such extension would prove empirically adequate is a question worth serious investigation. As I said at the outset, such an investigation would require a thorough consideration of data of the sort we have considered for 'that' phrases in the present work.

Against Ambiguity Approaches

It is time to address an issue that came up briefly in chapter
2. In defending the quantificational account ultimately
adopted there, I noted that it seemed preferable in various
respects to the other quantificational accounts scouted in
that chapter. It (along with another quantificational account discussed in chapter 2) was preferable to the first of
the three quantificational accounts discussed in that it
allowed uses of 'that' phrases involving perceptual intentions to be rigid, while allowing (usual) uses of 'that'
phrases involving descriptive intentions to be nonrigid. As
was mentioned, intuitively this seems the correct result.
However, this feature of my theory might incline some to
make the following sort of objection to it.[1]

If certain uses of 'that' phrases are rigid and certain
uses are not, why not think that this fact shows that
we should not even attempt to provide a unified semantic
account of these uses? What could be more different than
rigid and nonrigid noun phrases? Moreover, this isn't like
the case of definite descriptions, where the rigidity of some
descriptions can be attributed either to the presence of
something like 'actual' in the description ('the actual inventor of bifocals') or to predicative material in the description
that expresses a property whose extension does not vary
from possible world to possible world ('even prime number'). Because of this, descriptions that are rigid can trace

their rigidity to semantic features of linguistic expressions in them. Thus the fact that there are rigid and nonrigid descriptions is simply a consequence of the fact that descriptions can contain such expressions or not. And so the fact that there are rigid and nonrigid descriptions does not militate against providing a single semantic account for descriptions. For given expressions like 'actual' and 'even prime number', we can see that noun phrases that function semantically as do definite descriptions would have to include some noun phrases that are rigid. But this story cannot be told in the case of 'that' phrases. One and the same 'that' phrase can be rigid in one use (with perceptual intentions) and nonrigid in another (with descriptive intentions). Obviously, then, that some uses of 'that' phrases are rigid and others are not cannot be explained by reference to the semantic features of certain expressions occurring in the former, as can be done in the case of definite descriptions.

Thus, the objection continues, in the case of definite descriptions, given the way they function semantically, and given the semantics of 'actual' and expressions like 'even prime number', we would *expect* expressions that function the way descriptions do to include some noun phrases that are rigid. But there is no comparable explanation as to why expressions that function as we claim 'that' phrases do would include some rigid and some nonrigid noun phrases. In short, while there is a clear and principled explanation of why definite descriptions, though not ambiguous, are sometimes rigid and sometimes not, such an explanation is not available for 'that' phrases. It is simply a brute fact of our semantics that some uses are rigid and some are not. Thus, we have a gerrymandered theory that artificially cobbles together expressions that have nothing in common semantically and are only syntactically similar.

So the direct reference theorist in particular might respond to the data I have cited by saying that it was never her intention to account for the nonrigid (NDNS and some QI) uses we have discussed. Thus she could agree that the account I have provided is fine for such cases. She would only insist that I have given no evidence against her account of *rigid* uses, and that the present considerations suggest that we ought to adopt a theory of 'that' phrases according to which they are ambiguous. Thus, her account is to be maintained for rigid uses, and something like the present account ought to be adopted *only* for NDNS and (nonrigid) QI uses.[2] This objection to my view is an important one and it deserves a response. Providing a response is the business of the present chapter.

Let us think about the heart of the objection being made. First, in urging that we adopt an "ambiguity approach" to 'that' phrases, giving one semantic account for rigid uses and another for nonrigid uses, our objector plays up a semantic difference between some uses of 'that' phrases and others (some are rigid; others not) and at least implicitly claims that there are no similarities and hence nothing to suggest that all uses of 'that' phrases should fall under one theory. Second, she claims that my theory can give no principled explanation of the semantic difference she cites. She claims it is a brute fact in my theory that some uses of 'that' phrase are rigid and others are not. This is supposed to show that we really should prefer an ambiguity approach to my unified account.

But our objector is wrong on both counts. As I shall show, there *are* similarities in the behavior of rigid and nonrigid 'that' phrases, and these similarities suggest that a single semantic account should be given. And our account *does* give a principled explanation of why some uses of 'that' phrases are rigid and some are not. Finally, we shall show that there is some direct evidence against an ambiguity approach and in favor of a univocal account of 'that' phrases.

To begin, then, note that I have argued that there is a semantic feature that runs through *all* the uses of 'that' phrases under consideration. In particular, allowing supplementation by speaker's intentions (and the properties they determine) is a semantic feature that I have claimed is common to all these uses of 'that' phrases. Surely, if this is correct, it is strong prima facie evidence in favor of a univocal semantics for 'that' phrases. That an expression allows supplementation of this sort in a variety of uses is quite distinctive and suggestive. It should make us suspect that there is a *single* semantics for all such uses.

But have I really shown that 'that' phrases *do* allow supplementation of the sort described in all their uses? It certainly seems so. "Classic demonstrative" uses of 'that' phrases clearly allow some sort of supplementation; even many direct reference theorists agree that speakers intentions are relevant to the semantics of 'that' phrases in such uses. Of course, they think these intentions are relevant in a different way than I do. But the point is they agree that the semantics of 'that' phrases allows a supplementation by the speaker's intentions in a way that definite descriptions don't. The only philosophers who would disagree with this are direct reference theorists who think that it is the *demonstration*, and not the intention backing it, that is semantically relevant. But even here, they agree that 'that' phrases allow *some* sort of "extralinguistic" supplementation. So all parties agree that in classic demonstrative uses, 'that' phrases allow some sort of extralinguistic supplementation provided by the speaker. Thus, those who disagree with my view must admit that their disagreement with me here is extremely subtle, and concerns only what *form* is taken by the extralinguistic supplementation allowed by classic demonstrative uses of 'that' phrases. And I can think of no good reason for thinking that my account is less plausible than theirs on this point.

Further, in chapter 2, I gave a variety of arguments to show that there are QI and NDNS uses of 'that' phrases in which speakers' intentions are not redundant. But this is just another way of saying that such uses allow for semantically significant supplementation by properties determined by the speaker's intentions. Here it was particularly striking that the differences in the behavior of definite descriptions and 'that' phrases in classic demonstrative uses (i.e., 'That car is nicer than that car' is felicitous when I point at two different cars; 'The car is nicer than the car' is not, etc.) were also present when we compared definite descriptions to NDNS and QI uses of 'that' phrases (see chapter 2, examples (15)–(20) and the discussion preceding and following these examples). We took these differences of behavior to indicate that in *all these uses*, 'that' phrases allow supplementation by properties determined by the intentions of the speaker. That in classic demonstrative uses, QI uses, and NDNS uses the behavior of 'that' phrases would differ from that of definite descriptions *in the same ways* surely provides a powerful argument that the same sort of supplementation occurs in all these cases, and that we should give a unified semantic account of all these uses.

Thus, I have given good reason for thinking that all the uses of 'that' phrases considered here allow for supplementation by properties determined by the speaker's intentions. To repeat, the mere fact of allowing supplementation in all of its uses, and the corresponding differences of behavior between 'that' phrases *in all these uses* and definite descriptions, should make a univocal semantics prima facie much more plausible than one that posits an ambiguity, contrary to what the objection suggests. The objection, in ignoring this common semantic feature and common behavior of all uses of 'that' phrases and citing only semantic differences between various uses, makes the case for an ambiguity theory initially appear stronger than it is.

This leads to my second point. The semantic *difference* between various uses cited (some are rigid; others not) *does* have a clear, principled explanation on the present view. Indeed, the case of definite descriptions is not as disanalogous to the case of 'that' phrases as the objection claims it is. Of course, as I have already mentioned, unlike definite descriptions, one and the same 'that' phrase can be rigid in certain uses and not rigid in others. Thus the rigidity of certain uses in general cannot be traced to semantic properties of *linguistic expressions* occurring in the 'that' phrases, as can be done in the case of definite descriptions.[3] But the theory still offers a principled explanation of why some uses are rigid and others are not. As was just mentioned, the theory claims that all uses of 'that' phrases allow for completion or supplementation by properties determined by the intentions of speakers. Further, when we examine the various uses carefully, we note that they employ two importantly different kinds of intentions. And we find that which of the two intentions is employed correlates with whether the use is rigid or not.[4] In addition, there is a plausible story about why the different intentions determine different properties such that uses involving the one sort of intention are rigid, whereas uses involving the other sort are not. A perceptual intention is an intention to talk about the object b of one's perceptual intention. Thus it isn't surprising that such intentions would determine properties (being identical to b; and being jointly instantiated in w,t—the world and time of the context of utterance) that result in the proposition expressed being one whose truth conditions track the object b across worlds and times. By contrast, a descriptive intention is an intention to talk about the unique satisfier of some conjunction C of properties. Thus it isn't surprising that such an intention determines properties (possessing C; being jointly instantiated) that result in the proposition expressed choosing from a given circumstance of evaluation the satisfier of C there.

The upshot is that the rigidity of 'that' phrases, like that of definite descriptions, is traceable to particular elements involved in their interpretation. The only difference is that in the case of rigid descriptions, these elements are contributed by linguistic material in the descriptions (either 'actual' or an expression expressing a property whose extension is constant across possible worlds); whereas, in the case of 'that' phrases, because, unlike descriptions, their semantics allows for supplementation by properties determined by speakers' intentions, the rigidifying effect can come from *those* properties and hence not be traceable to any *linguistic expressions* in the 'that' phrases. Given the view that 'that' phrases in all their different uses allow such supplementation *and* that intentions in using 'that' phrases differ in the way claimed, we have a principled, plausible explanation of why some uses of 'that' phrases are rigid and others are not, even though 'that' phrases are not ambiguous.

In short, I have established that all uses of 'that' phrases under consideration allow supplementation of a certain sort. Though speaker intentions are the mechanism of supplementation in all uses, we find that there are two importantly different kinds of intentions speakers have in using 'that' phrases. These two kinds of intentions correlate with rigid and nonrigid uses, respectively. And I have explained why and how these intentions determine properties that, when supplementing the 'that' phrases, make some rigid and others not. Thus, the present univocal semantic theory explains in a principled way why some uses of 'that' phrases are rigid and others are not.

Indeed, it seems to me that the explanation is every bit as principled as the explanation of why some uses of definite descriptions are rigid and others are not. Whereas the latter explanation traces rigidity to the semantic properties of linguistic expressions occurring in the description, the former traces rigidity to features of the speaker's intentions that supplement the 'that' phrase and the sorts of properties they determine. Given that we have already established that the semantics of 'that' phrases allows for such supplementation, such an explanation is rather pleasing.

In thinking about this explanation, it is worth reflecting on QI uses. Here we have a use of a 'that' phrase that always contains a variable bound by a higher quantifier. But we find that QI uses sometimes involve perceptual intentions and sometimes involve descriptive intentions. They are rigid in the former case, and not in the latter. That we find rigid and nonrigid uses of 'that' phrases *within the category of QI uses*, and that the rigidity and lack of it correlate precisely with the different intentions mentioned, to my mind provides strong evidence in favor of the explanation offered.

I have couched my discussion of this issue in terms of a version of the theory according to which there are only *two* kinds of intentions that speakers have in using 'that' phrases. On this theory speakers either have a *descriptive intention*, an intention to talk about whatever it is that satisfies some property or conjunction of properties C; or they have a *perceptual intention*, an intention to talk about some object b they are perceiving. In the former case, it was claimed that the speaker is not trying to make a claim that tracks some particular object across worlds and times and so her intention also determines the property of being jointly instantiated. Thus her 'that' phrase is nonrigid. In the latter case, she is try to make such a claim that tracks a particular object (b) across worlds and time regardless of its possession of certain properties there. And so her intention also determines the property of being jointly instantiated in w,t (where w,t are the world and time of her context of utterance). But we saw in chapter 2 that there are versions of this view, which have not been ruled out, that allow that in using 'that' phrases speakers may have other kinds of intentions than just these two. The important point for the purposes of the present discussion is that even if one of these other versions of the present view is adopted, it would not affect the claim being made here that my theory explains in a principled way why some uses of 'that' phrases are rigid and others are not. For the crucial point here is that the rigidity and nonrigidity of uses of 'that' phrases is traceable to features of the speaker's intentions that supplement the 'that' phrases and the sorts of properties they determine. But this will be true on any version of the theory, no matter how many kinds of speakers intentions it claims are involved in using 'that' phrases. No matter how many kinds of intentions a given version of the view posits, whether a use of a 'that' phrase with a given sort of intention is rigid or not will be traceable to what that intention is like and what properties it determines. Thus, any version will give a principled explanation of why some uses of 'that' phrases are rigid and some are not.

Let me summarize the response thus far to the objection. First, I pointed out that the objection made the case for an ambiguity approach to 'that' phrases appear stronger than it is by pointing out differences in semantic features of certain uses of 'that' phrases (some are rigid, some are not) while failing to note that a common semantic feature runs through all uses (allowing for completion by properties determined by the intentions of the speaker) and by failing to note that *in all uses* the behavior of 'that' phrases differs from the behavior of definite descriptions *in the same way*. I noted that once this common feature and common behavior are recognized, a univocal semantics is prima facie more plausible than an ambiguity approach, exactly contrary to what the objection claims. Second, I refuted the objector's claim that since a univocal theory of definite descriptions can explain in a principled way why some definite descriptions are rigid and some are not and the present theory cannot explain in a principled way why some uses of 'that' phrases are rigid and some are not, a univocal semantics is plausible for the former but not the latter. In particular, the present account can give a principled explanation of why some uses of 'that' phrases are rigid and others are not.

Let me mention two final points in favor of the present account and against an account that holds that 'that' phrases are ambiguous, having quantificational uses and directly referential uses. In arguing against direct reference accounts in chapter 1, I noted that there are tests to determine whether a given NP undergoes movement in the mapping from S-structure to LF. Since it is generally held that quantifiers undergo movement and referring expressions do not, these tests can be used to determine which expressions are quantifiers. I noted in chapter 1 that these tests, when applied to 'that' phrases, indicate that they do undergo movement and so are quantificational. But more importantly for present concerns, when we perform these tests using classic demonstrative uses of 'that' phrases, the tests *still* show that the 'that' phrases undergo movement. But if the ambiguity hypothesis were correct, we should not expect this! If 'that' phrases really were ambiguous between referring and quantificational uses, we should expect referring uses not to show signs of movement and quantificational uses to indicate movement. Thus the following movement data strongly supports the view that

'that' phrases are univocally quantificational and so cuts strongly against ambiguity approaches.

Recall that it is a condition on VP deletion that neither the missing verb nor its antecedent c-commands the other. But as pointed out in chapter 1, examples involving quantifiers appear to violate this condition. For example, in

(1)   Tiger birdied every hole that Michael did,

'birdied' c-commands 'did'. However, if we assume that quantifier phrases are moved, resulting in their being adjoined to the S node at LF (leaving behind traces), 'birdied' will not c-command 'did' at LF as a result of the movement of 'every hole that Michael did'. Thus, to repeat what was said in chapter 1, if we assume that the constraint on VP must be satisfied only at the level of LF and that quantifier phrases are moved in the way suggested in the mapping to LF, examples like (1) don't constitute counterexamples to a well-motivated constraint on VP deletion. For present purposes, the crucial point is this. Supposes I am a sports broadcaster in a tower overlooking a golf course watching Tiger and Michael play golf. Suppose I am asked how Tiger is doing on the holes Michael birdied. Surely I can point at two holes successively and say

(2)   Tiger birdied that hole that Michael did but not that one.

That (2) is acceptable *even when the 'that' phrase is used with a perceptual intention and demonstration* strongly suggests that even in such uses 'that' phrases move in the mapping to LF and so are quantifier phrases.[5] Hence, contrary to what the objector claimed, we *do* here have evidence against her account of *rigid* uses of 'that' phrases. Her account cannot explain why such uses of 'that' phrases undergo movement that is characteristic of quantificational noun phrases.

Similarly, 'that' phrases used with perceptual intentions and demonstrations induce weak crossover effects just as do other quantifiers. Referring expressions, however, do not. Thus, the following sentence has no interpretation on which 'his' is anaphoric on 'every man' (i.e., no reading on which it means that every man is loved by his mother):

(3) His mother loves every man.

Similarly, if we use other quantifier phrases instead of 'every man', as before we don't get sentences in which the pronoun can be interpreted as anaphoric on the quantifier:

(3a) His mother loves some man.

(3b) His mother loves the man with the goatee.

(3c) His mother loves no man.

(3d) Their mothers love few men.

(3e) Their mothers love several men.

By contrast, if we replace the quantifier phrase with a name, we are able to interpret the pronoun as anaphoric on the name. Thus the following sentence has a reading on which it means that John's mother loves him:

(3′) His mother loves John.

Again, the usual explanations of weak crossover effects make essential reference to the fact that a quantifier phrase occurs in object position and, unlike a name, undergoes movement in the mapping to LF. Thus quantifiers in these constructions don't allow the anaphoric readings in question. Again, the crucial point for us is that 'that' phrases *used with perceptual intentions and demonstrations* behave like the quantifiers in (3a)–(3e). In particular, the pronoun in the following example cannot be understood as anaphoric on the 'that' phrase:

(3″)   His mother loves [pointing] that man with the goatee.[6]

To repeat, when we consult movement tests used to detect quantifier phrases using classic demonstrative uses of 'that' phrases, the tests show that the 'that' phrases undergo movement as only quantifiers do. But the ambiguity hypothesis should lead us to think this wouldn't be so. If 'that' phrases really were ambiguous, we should expect referring uses and quantificational uses to fare differently on these movement tests. But they don't. Again, this seems to me to provide significant support to the present view, which of course holds that all uses of 'that' phrases are quantificational.

Finally, there is the obvious methodological argument that a unified semantic account of a certain range of data is to be preferred to an account that posits an ambiguity in an expression in sentences comprising the data. Of course, if the unified account appears ad hoc or unprincipled in some way, this prima facie preference can be overridden. But in light of the arguments given in the present chapter, I think it can hardly be said that the unified account *is* ad hoc or unprincipled. Not only does it provide a principled explanation of why the relevant expressions sometimes exhibit importantly different semantic properties (i.e., rigidity and nonrigidity), but it also explains a fact (that syntactic movement tests come out the way that they do) that a theory that posits an ambiguity would have trouble explaining. Surely, in a case of this sort, general methodological procedure supports the theory that posits no ambiguity.

But now what if my account cannot be extended to apply to simple 'that' ('that' when used by itself as a demonstrative—see the discussion of simple 'that' in chapter 4)? Let's be pessimistic and assume it can't be. In particular, let's assume that *none* of the arguments against direct reference accounts of 'that' phrases goes through for simple 'that'; that there is *no* clear explanation as to why the quantificational theorist of simple 'that' should expect them not to go through (based on differences between simple 'that' and 'that' phrases that she would be prepared to admit); and that *all* extensions of my account to simple 'that' (including, but not limited to, those considered in chapter 4) prove empirically inadequate. Obviously, if this were to occur, we would have to claim that simple 'that' and 'that' as it occurs in 'that' phrases function differently semantically. So *we* would be committed to an ambiguity in 'that' (but not, of course, as it occurs in 'that' *phrases*). Let us further suppose that a direct reference account of simple 'that' is correct. In such a circumstance, what reason would there be, if any, to prefer the combination of our account of 'that' phrases and a direct reference account of simple 'that' to an ambiguity approach that holds that simple 'that' and rigid 'that' phrases refer directly and nonrigid 'that' phrases have some other semantics? Both approaches posit ambiguities in 'that'; they simply draw the line in different places. So the question is: which draws the line in the correct place and why?

If, as we are now imagining, the arguments against direct reference accounts of 'that' phrases fail to go through as arguments against a direct reference account of simple 'that', this means that movement tests and various arguments fail to support the claim that simple 'that' is quantificational. But we have seen that they *do* support the claim that 'that' phrases, *even those that are rigid and involve demonstrations*, are quantificational. Further, we have seen that the account I have sketched *can* handle rigid 'that' phrases used with demonstrations and that it makes correct predictions about such uses exhibiting scope interactions. But, as we are imagining things, *no* extension of our account can properly handle simple 'that'. *But then all of this constitutes evidence that 'that' phrases should be a semantically unified category and that simple 'that' should be handled differently*! For in the imagined situation, movement data, exhibition of scope interaction with other scoped elements, being capable of being treated by a semantic theory of a certain sort, and so on group rigid 'that' phrases (used with demonstrations) along with other uses of 'that' phrases and *fail* to group simple 'that' along with them. But then the independent evidence available *favors* the view that a unified semantic account is to be given for *'that' phrases* and a separate account is to be given for simple 'that' *over* the view that a unified semantic account is to be given of simple 'that' and rigid 'that' phrases used with demonstrations, with another semantic account being given for other uses of 'that' phrases.

Let me close this chapter and the present work by reminding the reader that we have no reason to be as pessimistic about the prospects for extending the account to simple 'that' as we have just pretended to be. It may well be that the account *can* be extended, along one of the lines suggested here or in some other way, to handle uses of simple 'that'. At this point, there is no real reason for pessimism about the possibility of such an extension. However, I have argued that even if this should not prove tenable, my account of 'that' *phrases* is superior to an ambiguity approach.

Appendix: Formal Semantics

We provide a formal semantics for a simple language containing complex 'that' phrases. Suppose our language contains n-place predicates ('A', 'B', with or without numerical subscripts) for all $n > 0$; individual variables ('x', 'y', with or without numerical subscripts); and names ('a', 'b', 'c'). It also contains a two-place identity predicate 'G' (I abbreviate formulas formed using this predicate by things like '$x = y$' for ease of readability). The language contains the determiners 'every', 'some', and 'that', and the modal operator 'P' ("possibly").

The syntax is as follows:

1. If δ is a determiner, α is a variable, and Σ is a formula containing free occurrences of α, $[\delta\alpha\Sigma]$ is a quantifier phrase.

2. If Π is an n-place predicate and $\alpha_1, \ldots, \alpha_n$ are names or variables, $[\Pi\alpha_1, \ldots, \alpha_n]$ is a formula.

3. If Ω is a quantifier phrase and Σ is a formula, then $[\Omega\Sigma]$ is a formula.

4. If Ψ and Φ are formulas, so are $\sim\Phi$ and $[\Phi \& \Psi]$.

5. If Ψ is a formula, so is $P[\Psi]$.

For each simple expression e of the language, we say what e *expresses*. With the exception of 'that', an expression contributes what it expresses to propositions expressed in a context by formulas containing it. I assume that the names of our language have bearers and that n-place predicates have been associated with n-place relations.

A simple expression e *expresses* e^* iff:

1. e is a variable and $e = e^*$.

2. e is a name and e^* is the bearer of e.

3. e is an n-place predicate and e^* is the n-place relation associated with e (we call 1-place relations *properties*). In particular, where e is '$=$', e^* is the two-place relation of identity.

4. e is the determiner 'every' or 'some', and e^* is the relation between properties EVERY (each instance of __ is an instance of __), or SOME (__ and __ have a common instance), respectively. (In fact, we shall take determiners to express relations between propositional frames—see below.)

5. e is the determiner 'that' and e^* is the relation THAT (i.e., __ and __ are uniquely __ in an object and it is __).

6. e is '$\sim$' or '$\&$' and e^* is the truth function NOT or AND, respectively.

7. e is 'P' and e^* is the property (of propositions) POSSIBLY (of being possible).

Assume we are given a set W of possible worlds; a set I of individuals (for simplicity, common to all the worlds); a set T of times (common to all the worlds); and a set C of contexts such that for each c in C, $c = \langle i,w,t \rangle$, where $i \in I$ (and is the *agent of c*), $w \in W$, and $t \in T$.

In what follows let δ be a determiner other than 'that'; Σ, Ψ, be formulas; Π be an n-place predicate; $\alpha_1, \alpha_2, \ldots$ be names or variables; and ξ be a variable. For any simple expression e, let e^* be what e expresses. Let c be the context $\langle i,w,t \rangle$.

We define the *propositional frame expressed by a formula in c*:

1. The propositional frame expressed by $[\Pi\alpha_1, \ldots, \alpha_n]$ in c is $[\Pi^* \alpha_1{}^*, \ldots, \alpha_n{}^*]$ (though I write "identity propositional frames" as, e.g., $[x^* =^* y^*]$).

2. The propositional frame expressed by $[[\delta\xi\Sigma]\Psi]$ in c is $[[\delta^*\xi\Sigma']\Psi']$, where Σ', Ψ' are the propositional frames expressed by Σ, Ψ in c respectively.

3. The propositional frame expressed by $[[\text{That}\xi\ \Sigma]\Psi]$ in c is $[[\text{THAT}_{f(c),h(c)}\ \xi\ \Sigma']\Psi']$, where f is a function from contexts to propositional frames and h is a function that maps each context $\langle i,w,t\rangle$ to *either* J, the property of being jointly instantiated, *or* J_{wt}, the property of being jointly instantiated in w,t, where if $f(c) = [\xi =^* o]$ or $[o =^* \xi]$, for some individual o, then $h(c) = \text{J}_{w,t}$. Otherwise, $h(c) = \text{J}$; and $\text{THAT}_{f(c),h(c)}$ is the result of saturating the second and third argument places in the 4-place relation expressed by 'that' (i.e., THAT: __ and __ are uniquely __ in an object and it is __) with $f(c)$ and $h(c)$ respectively (i.e., __ and $f(c)$ are uniquely jointly instantiated/jointly instantiated in w,t in an object and it is __); and with Σ', Ψ' as above.

4. The propositional frames expressed by $\sim\Sigma$ and $[\Sigma\&\Psi]$ in c are $\sim^*\Sigma'$ and $[\Sigma'\&^*\Psi']$, respectively, with Σ', Ψ' as above.

5. The propositional frame expressed by $[\text{P}[\Psi]]$ in c is $[\text{P}^* [\Psi']]$, Ψ' as above.

I call these *propositional frames* because they include things like $[\Pi^*x]$, (where Π^* is a property and x is a variable), which contain free variables. Propositions are propositional frames containing no free variables.[1] Clause 3 requires a little explanation. The function f maps contexts to propositional frames. Intuitively, where $c = \langle i,w,t\rangle$, the propositional frame $f(c)$ represents the property or relation determined by the intention of the agent of c (i.e., i) at t in w that saturates the second argument place of the four-place relation expressed by 'that' and so further restricts the quantification expressed by the 'that' phrase. The function h maps a context $c = \langle i,w,t \rangle$ to either the property of being jointly instantiated or the property of being jointly instantiated in w,t (depending on what f maps c to), which then saturates the third argument place in the four-place relation expressed by 'that'. I note that we don't allow a bunch of different fs and hs here. We take it to be a matter of fact which properties are determined by an agent i's intentions at w,t for all contexts $\langle i,w,t \rangle$, and (the particular) f and h encode these facts.[2]

Let g be a function that maps variables to individuals ($\in I$) and individuals to themselves; $\psi_1, \psi_2, \ldots$ be individuals or variables; ξ be a variable; R be an n-place relation ($1 \leq n$); and Ξ, Γ, Θ be propositional frames.

Where Δ is a propositional frame, we define *the proposition expressed by Δ relative to g*, $Pr(\Delta)_g$, as follows:

1. If $\Delta = [R\ \psi_1, \ldots, \psi_n]$, then $Pr(\Delta)_g = [R\ g(\psi_1), \ldots, g(\psi_n)]$

2. If $\Delta = [[\text{EVERY } \xi\ \Xi]\ \Gamma]$ (recall that EVERY is the relation between properties: each instance of __ is an instance of __), then $Pr(\Delta)_g = [[\text{EVERY } \xi\ Pr(\Xi)_{g\text{-}\xi}]\ Pr(\Gamma)_{g\text{-}\xi}]$, where $Pr(\Omega)_{g\text{-}\xi}$, for Ω a propositional frame, is the result of replacing $g(\xi)$ by ξ in $Pr(\Omega)_g$, (similar clause for SOME).

3. If $\Delta = [[\text{THAT}_{\Theta,J^*}\ \xi\ \Xi]\Gamma]$ (where J^* is the property of being jointly instantiated or the property of being jointly instantiated in w,t, for some world and time w,t), $Pr(\Delta)_g = [[\text{THAT}_{Pr(\Theta)g\text{-}\xi,J^*}\ \xi\ Pr(\Xi)_{g\text{-}\xi}]\ Pr(\Gamma)_{g\text{-}\xi}]$, $Pr(\Omega)_{g\text{-}\xi}$, for Ω a propositional frame, as in 2.

4. If $\Delta = [\Xi \text{ AND } \Gamma]$ (recall that AND is the truth function for conjunction), $Pr(\Delta)_g = [Pr(\Xi)_g \text{ AND } Pr(\Gamma)_g]$, (similar clause for negation).

5. If $\Delta = [\text{POSSIBLY}[\Xi]]$, then $Pr(\Delta)_g = [\text{POSSIBLY}[Pr(\Xi)_g]]$. (Note that if Δ has no free variables (i.e., is a proposition), then $Pr(\Delta)_g = \Delta$.)

Let $o, o^1, o^2, \ldots$ be individuals; g, g' be functions that map variables to individuals and individuals to themselves; R be an n-place relation; Ξ, Γ, Θ be propositional frames; X, Y be propositions; and ξ be a variable. If R is an n-place relation, the *intension of R* is a function from world-time pairs to sets of n-tuples of individuals; and the *extension of R in w,t*, $\text{ext}_{w,t}(R)$, is the result of applying its intension to the world-time pair w,t. Finally, as suggested above, we will take determiners to express relations between propositional frames with one free variable (instead of properties).[3]

1. A proposition of the form $[R\, o^1, \ldots, o^n]$ is true in w,t iff $\langle o^1, \ldots, o^n \rangle$ belongs to $\text{ext}_{w,t}(R)$.

2. A proposition of the form $[[\text{EVERY}\ \xi\ \Xi]\Gamma]$ is true in w,t iff $\{o^1$: for some g' such that $g'(\xi) = o^1$, $Pr(\Xi)_{g'}$ is true in $w,t\}$ is a subset of $\{o$: for some g such that $g(\xi) = o$, $Pr(\Gamma)_g$ is true in $w,t\}$ (similar clauses for SOME—this may make it appear as though EVERY is a three-place relation between two propositional frames and a world-time pair w,t; but I take EVERY to be a 2-place relation between propositional frames that obtains at some world-time pairs and not at others).

3. A proposition of the form $[[\text{THAT}_{\Theta, J} \cdot \xi\ \Xi]\Gamma]$ is true in w,t iff

case 1: $J^* = J$ (the property of being jointly instantiated): $\{o$: for some g such that $g(\xi) = o$, $Pr(\Theta)_g$ and $Pr(\Xi)_g$ are true in $w,t\}$ has one member o^1 and $o^1\ \varepsilon\ \{o$: for some g' such that $g'(\xi) = o$, $Pr(\Gamma)_{g'}$ is true in $w,t\}$.

case 2: $J^* = J_{w't'}$ (the property of being jointly instantiated in w',t', for some w',t'): $\{o$: for some g such that $g(\xi) = o$, $Pr(\Theta)_g$ and $Pr(\Xi)_g$ are true in $w',t'\}$ has one member o^1 and

$o^1 \, \varepsilon \, \{o$: for some g' such that $g'(\xi) = o$, $Pr(\Gamma)_{g'}$ is true in $w,t\}$.

4. A proposition of the form [X AND Y] is true in w,t iff the value of AND when applied to the truth values of X and Y in w,t is true (similar clause for negation).

5. A proposition of the form [POSSIBLY[X]] is true in w,t iff for some w', X is true in w',t.

The formula [[Thatξ Σ]Ψ] in c expresses the propositional frame [[THAT$_{f(c),h(c)}$ ξ Σ']Ψ'], where Σ' and Ψ' are the propositional frames expressed by Σ and Ψ in c, respectively. The formula [[Thatξ Σ]Ψ&Σ] in c expresses the propositonal frame [[THAT$_{f(c),h(c)}$ ξ Σ']Ψ' AND Σ']. We wish to consider (CIC) (see chapter 4) for formulas such as these that express propositions (i.e., propositional frames without free variables).

Thus suppose the formula [[Thatξ Σ]Ψ] in $c = \langle i,w,t \rangle$ expresses the proposition [[THAT$_{f(c),h(c)}$ ξ Ξ]Γ] and that the formula [[Thatξ Σ]Ψ&Σ] in $c = \langle i,w,t \rangle$ expresses the proposition [[THAT$_{f(c),h(c)}$ ξ Ξ][ΓAND Ξ]] (where, as before, Γ and Ξ are propositional frames). Then we want to show:

(CIC)   [[THAT$_{f(c),h(c)}$ ξ Ξ]Γ] is true in w,t iff [[THAT$_{f(c),h(c)}$ ξ Ξ][ΓAND Ξ]] is true in w,t.

(The crucial point is that w,t, the world and time of evaluation, are the world and time of the context c.)

PROOF: Whether $h(c) = J_{wt}$ (being jointly instantiated in w,t) or $=J$ (being jointly instantiated) will not matter in this case. As can be seen by looking at the two cases (corresponding to whether $J^* = J_{wt}$ or J) in semantic clause 3 in the previous definition, these cases collapse into one when the world and time of the context is the world and time at which the proposition is being evaluated. Suppose [[THAT$_{f(c),h(c)}$ ξ Ξ]Γ] is true in w,t.

Then $\{o$: for some g such that $g(\xi) = o$, $Pr(f(c))_g$ and $Pr(\Xi)_g$ are true in $w,t\}$ has one member o^1 and o^1 ε $\{o$: for some g' such that $g'(\xi) = o$, $Pr(\Gamma)_{g'}$ is true in $w,t\}$. Consider a g such that $g(\xi) = o^1$, and $Pr(f(c))_g$ and $Pr(\Xi)_g$ are true in w,t; and a g' such that $g'(\xi) = o^1$, $Pr(\Gamma)_{g'}$ is true in w,t. Because $[[\text{THAT}_{f(c),h(c)} \; \xi \; \Xi]\Gamma]$ is a proposition (i.e., contains no free variables), we know that ξ is the only free variable in $f(c)$, Ξ, and Γ. But then since g and g' agree on ξ (both assign it o^1), $Pr(\Xi)_g$ is the same as $Pr(\Xi)_{g'}$. Thus $Pr(\Xi)_{g'}$ and $Pr(\Gamma)_{g'}$ are true in w,t. Hence $Pr([\Gamma \text{AND} \; \Xi])_{g'}$ is true in w,t. But then $\{o$: for some g such that $g(\xi) = o$, $Pr(f(c))_g$ and $Pr(\Xi)_g$ are true in $w,t\}$ has one member o^1 and o^1 ε $\{o$: for some g' such that $g'(\xi) = o$, $Pr([\Gamma \text{AND} \; \Xi])_{g'}$ is true in $w,t\}$. Thus $[[\text{THAT}_{f(c),h(c)} \; \xi \; \Xi] [\Gamma \text{AND} \; \Xi]]$ is true in w,t.

Suppose $[[\text{THAT}_{f(c),h(c)} \; \xi \; \Xi] [\Gamma \text{AND} \; \Xi]]$ is true in w,t. Then $\{o$: for some g such that $g(\xi) = o$, $Pr(f(c))_g$ and $Pr(\Xi)_g$ are true in $w,t\}$ has one member o^1 and o^1 ε $\{o$: for some g' such that $g'(\xi) = o$, $Pr([\Gamma \text{AND} \; \Xi])_{g'}$ is true in $w,t\}$. But then o^1 ε $\{o$: for some g' such that $g'(\xi) = o$, $Pr(\Gamma)_{g'}$ is true in $w,t\}$. Thus $[[\text{THAT}_{f(c),h(c)} \; \xi \; \Xi]\Gamma]$ is true in w,t.   Q.E.D.

Notes

Introduction

1

Of course Kaplan himself was more concerned with the *word* 'that' occurring by itself as a noun phrase ('That is a planet') than with what I am calling 'that' phrases. But Kaplan (1977) suggests that his account is to be extended to complex noun phrases, when, after characterizing the character of a complete demonstrative (a demonstrative completed by a demonstration), he says: "Obvious adjustments are to be made to take into account any common noun phrase which accompanies *or is built-in to the demonstrative*" (p. 527; my emphasis). Further, other philosophers have taken Kaplan's account to apply to what I call complex 'that' phrases.

2

Concerning differences of detail, see, e.g., Braun (1994), (1996); for dissent from the orthodoxy, see Lepore and Ludwig (2000), Neale (1993), and Richard (1993). Since for the most part I won't be explicitly criticizing these views in the present work, let me briefly say something about them. Though I would make a variety of detailed criticisms of each of them, there is one central and important criticism that applies to all of them. None of them, and no view known to me, can handle all uses of 'that' phrases discussed in the present work. This, together with the fact that the view I will eventually defend here *can* do this, seems to me a very powerful argument in its favor.

Chapter One

1

Though Kaplan (1977) talks a lot about this conception of propositions, he does not officially adopt it as part of his theory. See

p. 496. However, most current direct reference theorists do adopt this account of propositions. See King (1994, 1995, 1996) for a defense of a particular version of this kind of view of propositions.

2
I use 'talk about' here as a way of avoiding saying that the phrase *directly refers* to the thing talked about, since I don't think it does. Hence on my use to say that a phrase is used to talk about an individual does not commit one to the claim that the individual is contributed to the proposition expressed by the sentence containing the phrase.

3
Presumably, in such cases the descriptive material combined with 'that' in forming the 'that' phrase would have to determine the phrase's character by itself, since a demonstration and the sort of intention that accompanies a demonstration are lacking.

4
That is, the classmate does not employ a demonstration, need not be talking about anyone in the physical context of utterance, and has no particular individual in mind.

5
David Braun (in a personal communication regarding a different example) suggested this strategy. I take it Braun's suggestion is based on Kaplan's (1977) remarks on p. 560, footnote 76, where the same idea is discussed.

6
An anonymous referee claimed not to have the intuition that (2) is true in our altered situation. The final strategy discussed below for arguing that the intuition that (2) is true in the situation described is not a problem for the direct reference theorist was also suggested by a (different) anonymous referee.

7
Further, the answer to the (somewhat awkward) question 'Could that hominid who discovered how to start fires have failed to be that hominid who discovered how to make fires?' (where the 'that' phrases have NDNS uses) is 'yes'! Or at least informants who think the answer to the question 'Could the hominid who discovered how to start fires have failed to be the hominid who discovered how to start fires?' is 'yes', think the answer to the former is 'yes' as well. (Some have a hard time getting the reading of the *latter* on which the answer is 'yes'.) And that this is so shows that the 'that' phrases here have variable scope (with respect to the modal operator) and are nonrigid, just like definite descriptions. The former sentence (containing 'that' phrases) is admittedly more

awkward than the latter (containing definite descriptions), which clouds judgments here to some extent. The awkwardness appears to result from repetition of the 'that' phrase—consideration of simple examples suggests that repetition of a 'that' phrase in a clause or in closely related clauses with the intention to "pick out" the same thing both times often produces some awkwardness. For those who have trouble making judgments about this sentence ('Could that hominid ...') because of its awkwardness, note that 'Could that hominid who discovered how to start fires have failed to be Homey?' and 'Could Homey have failed to be that hominid who discovered how to start fires?' *clearly* have readings (the most natural ones) on which the answer is 'yes'. But (assuming Homey is the hominid who discovered how to start fires and that 'Homey' rigidly designates him) on these readings the 'that' phrase must be nonrigid (and take narrow scope with respect to the modal operator). I shall later briefly address the question of whether *all* NDNS uses of 'that' phrases (barring certain exceptional cases) are nonrigid. (If, for whatever reason, you don't like the present example, consider a professor lecturing on great moments in the history of clothing who doesn't know who invented the zipper but who has great admiration for him. Suppose he says 'That clothier who invented the zipper was a genius' and run the same argument.) See also the discussion of the interaction of NDNS uses and modal operators in chapter 3 (examples (2) and (3) and the surrounding discussion) for additional evidence that (at least some) NDNS uses are not rigid.

8

Neale (1993) denies that such constructions are possible, noting the unnaturalness of 'Every driver knows that mechanic working for him'. (Curiously, Neale also provides a perfectly acceptable instance of such a construction: 'Every man eagerly looks forward to that day when he retires', attributing it to Jamie Tappenden.) I agree with Neale that some such examples seem unnatural. However, many examples of this sort seem perfectly fine, as (4), (5) and the example in the present note indicate. What produces the unnaturalness in certain cases is an interesting question.

9

Above I said that these uses are closely related to QI uses. In fact, it is plausible to suppose that *at the level of LF*, they *are* QI uses. For example, the NS reading of (6) is likely produced by movement of the quantifiers in (6) in the mapping to LF (discussed below), so that *one* LF representation associated with (6) (the ambiguity in (6) noted in the text results from (6) having *other* LF representations associated with it as well) is (roughly):

(6a) [[[Each division: *x*] [[That professor who brought in the biggest grant in *x*: *y*] [*y* will be honored]]].

Here, of course, the quantifier 'Each division' binds a variable ('*x*'—a "trace" left from the movement of 'Each division') in the 'that' phrase. Thus, the difference between QI uses and NS readings may simply be (and, I think, is) that in the former there is an overt pronoun in the 'that' phrase that is bound by the higher quantifier whereas in the latter there is a trace/variable that does not appear in surface structure bound by the higher quantifier.

10
Of course, there are direct reference views that deny any semantic role to the predicative material combined with 'that' in forming a 'that' phrase. However, such views are very implausible in the present case. For we can imagine that the 'that' phrases have NDNS uses in (11) (indeed, this is the natural way to take (11)). Thus they are not accompanied by any demonstration, need not pick out anything in the physical context of utterance, and the speaker need have no particular things in mind as the "things she wants to talk about" (thus she might know just on general grounds that the person being addressed has a unique friend who has been studying for a unique exam she has been dreading). But since there is no demonstration in such a case, what *other than the predicative material in the 'that' phrases* could determine the characters, and hence the referents, of the 'that' phrases?

11
The direct reference theorist might attempt to get around the argument here by altering her view to allow two (or more) 'that' phrases to have their characters "simultaneously determind," in some way similar to the way in which we can simultaneously solve a system of equations for two variables. Obviously, such a semantics would be one in which other linguistic expressions could partly determine the character of a 'that' phrase; and, more specifically, in which two 'that' phrases *e* and *e'* could each play a role in simultaneously determining the character of the other. Pursuing such a strategy would clearly require a *huge* complication in the usual Kaplan-style direct reference account of 'that' phrases. Without attempting to actually formulate a semantics of this sort, it is very hard to picture what such a thing would look like. Thanks to Zoltan Gendler Szabo for raising this point.

12
Chomsky (1981), (1982); May (1985).

13
The following discussion leans heavily on May (1985). May uses "movement tests" tests to support the claim that definite descriptions are quantificational. See pp. 4–25.

14

Roughly, α c-commands β iff the first branching node dominating α dominates β and α does not dominate β.

15

A tree for (17) would look something like this:

Tiger   birdied   every hole that Michael did

(where I haven't bothered with the structure of 'every hole that Michael did', since it is apparent that 'birdied' c-commands 'did' without going into this).

16

Compare (18) with:

*(18a)   Copp flunked Holmes, who Jubien did.

*(18b)   Copp flunked him, who Jubien did.

These violate the condition on VP deletion even at LF, since 'Holmes' and 'him' are not quantifier phrases and so do not undergo movement. May (1985) defends the view that the acceptability of (17) (and (18)—in a personal communication), and the unacceptability of (18a) and (18b), are to be explained in terms of quantificational NPs' undergoing movement in the mapping to LF and referring expressions' not being subject to such movement. This explanation of the data has been challenged recently by Norbert Hornstein (1995). Hornstein argues that the acceptability of (17) and (18) and the unacceptability of (18a) and (18b) is not to be explained by appeal to a movement rule that applies to quantificational NPs and not names. If Hornstein is correct, then the acceptability of (18) does not show that the 'that' phrase in it is a quantifier phrase. Similarly, Larson and Ludlow (1993) claim that names optionally undergo movement of the sort I have supposed quantifiers undergo in examples like (17). So again, if they are right, the acceptability of (18) may show that 'that' phrases too undergo such movement, but it would not show that they are quantifiers (since nonquantifiers can undergo such movement). I have neither the time nor the space in the present work to defend May's account against the challenges of Hornstein and Larson and Ludlow. Let me, then, simply note that this argument depends on May's account of (17) and (18) and more generally on the idea that "movement tests" detect quantificational NPs. I am indebted to Peter Ludlow for bringing these issues to my attention.

17
For example, see May (1985), chapter 5. Thanks to Mandy Simons for discussion of and suggestions concerning weak cross-over data.

18
It is important that the pointing occur only when I utter the final word of the sentence, because if I point as I utter sentence-initial 'his', sentence-final 'him' can be interpreted as anaphoric on sentence-initial 'his'. But this is cheating! We have an anaphoric connection between 'him' and 'his', but 'him' is the anaphor, not the antecedent here. I find it helps to get the reading I am imagining to de-stress sentence-initial 'his' and stress 'him' as the pointing occurs.

19
Or at any rate, $(19'')$ on the interpretation in question sounds no better than $(19b)$. And both sound significantly worse (on the reading in question) than $(19')$. I am perfectly happy if, with respect to weak crossover effects, etc., the behavior of 'that' phrases resembles that of definite descriptions. For most take the latter to be quantifier phrases. See the next note.

20
'That' phrases sometimes appear not to display weak crossover effects. Thus 'Someone who liked her asked that woman wearing a red jacket to the dance' has a reading on which 'her' is anaphoric on 'that woman wearing a red jacket', whereas 'Someone who liked her asked every woman wearing a red jacket to the dance' does not have a reading on which 'her' is anaphoric on 'every woman wearing a red jacket'. Thus here 'every woman wearing a red jacket' exhibits weak crossover effects and 'that woman wearing a red jacket' doesn't. Exactly why this occurs is not clear. But in any case, it does not constitute evidence that 'that' phrases are not quantificational. For other phrases that most philosophers of language take to be quantifier phrases exhibit the same behavior as 'that' phrases in these constructions. In particular, 'Someone who liked her asked the woman wearing a red jacket to the dance' has a reading on which 'her' is anaphoric on the definite description 'the woman wearing the red jacket', which most philosophers of language take to be a quantifier phrase.

Chapter Two

1
King (1999).

2

Of course some determiners are syntactically singular (e.g., 'every') and some are plural (e.g., 'most'); and the syntactic number of the N′ constituent in a quantifier phrase must match the syntactic number of the determiner. Throughout the present work I adhere to the traditional view that quantifier phrases are to be syntactically analyzed as NPs, even though it is increasingly common to analyze them as determiner phrases. I don't believe anything I say hinges on which analysis is correct.

3

As discussed briefly below, in much of the literature on generalized quantifiers, determiners express or have as their denotations functions from sets of individuals to sets of sets of individuals. This is because the authors are looking at formal languages that are much like the standard first-order predicate calculus except in that they contain generalized quantifiers. And they are providing an extensional truth-conditional semantics for these languages that is similar to the standard semantics for first-order predicate calculus. But once we try to assign *structured propositions* to sentences of a language containing quantificational NPs, having determiners express relations between properties seems the natural approach. See note 5 below.

4

This isn't quite *my* view, because I hold that a syntactically complex N′ constituent, predicate nominal, or adjectival phrase contributes to propositions a complex entity I call a *propositional frame*. See King (1994, 1995, 1996) for discussion. But I do not wish to get bogged down in the details of my views about propositions here, since nothing hangs on it.

5

Here we can see why it is natural to treat determiners as contributing to propositions relations between *properties* (as opposed to sets). For 'Every woman is smart' expresses a proposition that is true at some possible worlds and false at others. On the present view, this is because the property expressed by 'woman' stands in the relation expressed by 'every' to the property expressed by 'smart' at some worlds and not at others. This, in turn, is a result of the fact that the properties expressed by 'woman' and 'smart' are differently instantiated in different worlds.

6

Of course, one might adopt a different treatment of quantification from the one I am discussing *across the board*. But the point is that a quantificational account of 'that' phrases ought to hold that the propositional contribution of 'that' is of the same ontological category as that of other determiners. Also, the claim suggested in the text that *all* determiners contribute *two*-place relations between properties to propositions is too strong. There are determiners that express, e.g., *three*-place relations between properties ('more __ than __' in sentences like 'More *A*s than *B*s are *C*s'). However, if 'that' is a determiner, it certainly appears to be one like 'every', 'some', etc. that contributes a two-place relation between properties to propositions. Thus I have focused on determiners of this sort. Finally, when I say that a quantificational account of 'that' phrases that doesn't hold that 'that' contributes to propositions a relation of the same category (i.e., a two-place relation between properties) as do other determiners will end up claiming that 'that' phrases (and/or their syntactic constituents) are *extremely* different from "ordinary" quantifier phrases either syntactically or semantically or both, I have in mind the following. Such a view must hold either: (1) that 'that' phrases, like structurally similar quantifiers ('every *F*', 'some *F*', etc), have the form Det+N' and that 'that' in 'that *F*' is a determiner, but it makes a contribution to propositions that is of a different sort than is made by determiners in structurally similar quantifier phrases; or (2) that 'that' phrases, though quantifier phrases, do not have the form Det+N' at all. If one holds (1), then one is forced to claim that determiners in what appear to be structurally similar phrases function differently semantically. As I suggested, it seems to me that one should avoid such a claim if one can. And I shall argue that one can! But further, if the *phrase* Det+N', where Det is 'that', functions *semantically* as do other quantifier phrases (and if not, in what sense is it a quantifier phrase at all?), obviously some account must be given of how phrases of the form Det+N' all function semantically in the same way, even though Det's function in two different semantic ways. And if one holds (2), one is making a syntactic proposal to the effect that quantifier phrases that appear to be structurally similar ('every *F*', 'some *F*' and 'that *F*') in fact have two different syntactic structures. But then there should be syntactic evidence of these different syntactic structures; and one wants to know what that evidence is. Further, again an account is owed of how these different syntactic structures both have the semantics of quantifier phrases.

As an apparent example of this second view, consider the view of Lepore and Ludwig (2000). On their view of 'that' phrases, sentences containing them express quantified claims. But they hold that 'that' in 'that *F*' is not a determiner but a (referring) NP. So on their view, 'That *F*' in 'That *F* is *G*' is the concatenation of the referring expression 'That' and the N' '*F*'. Thus, syntactically, it would appear to have the status of 'He student' in the ungrammatical sentence (uttered as I point at a male in front of me) 'He student is happy'. As a result, I think it is a bit of a mystery why 'That *F* is *G*' is even *grammatical* on their view (or why 'He student' isn't). In any case, Ludwig and Lepore apparently hold that the concatenation of a referring NP ('that') and an N′ constituent ('man in the corner') is a quantificational NP (though the concatenation of other referring NPs, e.g., 'he', and N′ constituents, e.g., 'student' fail to be NPs, let alone quantificational NPs). So Ludwig and Lepore are proposing that quantifier phrases that appear to be structurally similar have two very different syntactic structures: (1) the usual Det+N′ → NP; and their new (2) NP+N′ → NP (where only a *very* restricted class of NPs can combine with N′s to produce NPs). But then, as suggested above, one wants to know whether there is syntactic evidence to support the claim that quantificational NPs have these two different syntactic structures. In addition, as suggested above, Lepore and Ludwig owe an account of how and why the combination of a *referring expression* ('that') and an N′ (sometimes!) yields a phrase that semantically functions as a *quantifier phrase*. This also seems somewhat mysterious to me.

7
Given the way I have formulated my semantics, one can't assign names and quantifier phrases denotations of the same sort for the simple reason that I have not assigned denotations to quantifier phrases at all. Instead, I have assigned denotations (more or less, two-place relations between properties—see previous note) to *determiners*, and the propositions expressed by sentences containing a (wide scope) quantifier are true iff the property expressed by the N′ portion of the quantifier phrase stands in the relation expressed by the determiner to the property expressed by the rest of the sentence. But one could reformulate an account in the spirit of mine that does assign denotations to quantifier phrases, and one could then assign proper names denotations of the same sort. Again, this is not very interesting.

8
Actually, I think sometimes one *can* use two occurrences of 'the *F*' in the same sentences to "talk about" distinct *F*s. The point here is simply that sometimes one can't.

9
Kaplan originally took demonstrations to be relevant to determining the referents of 'that' phrases. But he later took the "directing intention" to be relevant and regarded the demonstration "as a mere *externalization* of this inner intention" (Kaplan 1989, p. 582). Thus I side with the later Kaplan on this point.

10

I should add that a quantificational account could in principle lack this feature. But obviously I think the best quantificational accounts possess this feature. Indeed, it was when I thought of handling speakers' intentions in the way described below that I first thought that a quantificational account of 'that' phrases might be correct.

11

King (1999).

12

In chapter 4 I will discuss how the sort of saturation discussed here, which "restricts" the quantification expressed by a 'that' phrase, differs from the phenomenon whereby a speaker utters 'Every student in the class is here' and thereby conveys the proposition that every student *in a particular class* is here.

13

The property determined by Danielle's intention in such a case still saturates an argument place in the four-place relation expressed by 'that'. It just does so to no semantic effect, since that very property is expressed by the predicative material she combined with 'that' in forming the 'that' phrase.

14

I was aware of this problem when I wrote King (1999) and hinted at it in note 21 of that paper. But for reasons I can no longer reconstruct, I thought the difficulty might be only apparent. I had always intended to investigate various quantificational approaches further, which is why I called the theory in King (1999) a "first approximation" to the correct account. My thought was that I would sort these things out in later work. Thus the present monograph.

15

See King (1999), pp. 169–171 for discussion. I shall also discuss QI uses and redundant intentions a bit later in the present work.

16

See King (1999), pp. 169–171 for discussion.

17

The notion of rigidity (and nonrigidity) being used here has to be relativized to an assignment of values to free variables. The point is that when we evaluate the 'that' phrase in (4) (really, its propositional contribution) at two different worlds w and w', even if the same professor is assigned to the variable/pronoun 'his/hers', the 'that' phrase may designate different publications. This violates the relativized notion of rigidity.

18
It is easy to show that being jointly instantiated and being jointly instantiated at w,t are distinct by looking at their extensions across possible worlds. Thus, let properties P and Q be jointly instantiated at w,t (and no other properties are jointly instantiated there) and let no properties be jointly instantiated at w',t'. Then at w',t', the extension of *being jointly instantiated* is the empty set; but the extension at w',t' of *being jointly instantiated at w,t* is $\{\langle P, Q \rangle\}$ (I assume, of course, that P and Q exist at w',t').

19
See the discussion of the interaction of NDNS uses and modal operators in chapter 3 (examples (2) and (3) and the surrounding discussion) for additional evidence that (at least some) NDNS uses are not rigid. As I mentioned before, I shall later briefly address the issue of whether all NDNS uses of 'that' phrases are nonrigid. Finally, let me add that depending on how finely one individuates propositions, it may be that the propositions T1 and T2 claim are expressed in this case are distinct. On a view of propositions of the sort I favor, the propositions in question certainly would be distinct.

20
We shall see in chapter 3 that when 'that' phrases combine with what are usually called *monotone decreasing* quantifiers (which 'every skier' is not), the quantifier scope ambiguity *does* give rise to two truth-conditionally different readings. It is worth noting that T1 and T2 make slightly different predictions in the case of (6), since (6a)/(6b) and (6c)/(6d) have slightly different truth conditions. For (6a)/(6b) to be true at an arbitrary world w', KT-22 must be a mountain at w'. For (6c)/(6d) to be true at w', KT-22 must be a mountain at w (the world of the context of utterance). Though it is hard to see in this example for a number of reasons, I shall later argue that T2 is correct.

21
Actually, I don't think this is a two-place relation. Rather it is a complex propositional constituent, which I call a *propositional frame* in the appendix, consisting of the "conjunctive combination" of the two-place kissing relation and the property of being a woman. However, the crucial point here is that this complex entity has two argument places. I have represented the proposition expressed by (7) somewhat differently than I have other propositions (e.g., (6c) and (6d)) because I am trying to make clear the nature of the propositional contribution of things like 'woman he kissed'.

22
Of course, this relation is also determined by the speaker's redundant intentions in this case. I have suppressed the redundancy in saying what proposition is expressed by (8) in the situation described to enhance comprehensibility. The proposition expressed really is the proposition that for most avid skiers x, the unique instance y of being the first black diamond run x attempted and being the first black diamond run x attempted, is such that x remembers y. Obviously, the truth conditions of this proposition and the one mentioned in the body are the same.

23
Or, without redundancy suppressed, for most avid snow skiers x, being the first black diamond run x attempted to ski and being the first black diamond run x attempted to ski are jointly instantiated in y, and x remembers y.

24
I find that (11) and examples like it strongly encourage an epistemic reading of the modal operator according to which an epistemic possibility is being asserted. I want to consider a reading of the modal operator where it expresses metaphysical modality, and I find inserting the modal auxiliary 'should have been' serves to suppress the epistemic reading of the modal.

25
Kripke (1980) uses an argument similar to the argument here involving (11′) against the view that names abbreviate definite descriptions that take wide scope over modal operators (see pp. 13–14). The arguments given against (T1) here also apply to the view of Lepore and Ludwig (2000). Indeed, in commenting on a version of their paper at the Pacific Division Meeting of the American Philosophical Association in 1998 I gave the argument concerning the missing reading (11b) of (11) against their view. I also gave the anticipated response noted in the text (concerning the pragmatic explanation of why (11) does not have the reading (11b)), and my response to this response given in the text. Lepore and Ludwig mention this objection in their paper (footnote 33) and give the response that I anticipated and responded to in my comments on their paper. They do not comment on my response, however. In any case, as noted in the text, even if we accepted the explanation of why (11) lacks the reading (11b) offered by Lepore and Ludwig and the (T1) theorist (though we shouldn't!), they still cannot explain why the second sentence of (11′) is not true in the described situation.

In short, the exact considerations that favor (T2) over (T1) also favor (T2) over the theory of Lepore and Ludwig. And indeed,

(T1) seems to me superior to their theory in that, unlike theirs, it handles QI and NDNS uses.

Finally, I should note that the arguments Ludwig and Lepore give against quantificational accounts of 'that' phrases (see section 3 of their paper) do not work against (T2). Thus, they overstate when, after giving those arguments, they say: "The case against treating complex demonstrative expressions as quantifiers seems decisive" (2000, p. 18).

26
Richard doesn't actually talk about perceptual intentions, etc., since this is my terminology. But it is clear that Richard is imagining standard "demonstrative" uses of the 'that' phrases in question.

27
Richard notes that this same problem arises for standard direct reference treatments of 'that' phrases.

28
Before turning away from T2's treatment of classic demonstrative uses of 'that' phrases, let me mention and respond to an objection to T2 raised by David Braun. (I seem to remember that at the conference on pragmatics and semantics at Cornell University in 1999, Alex Byrne raised a related objection to T2s predecessor in King (1999), to which the objection also applies. Alex isn't certain whether I am remembering correctly or not.) Suppose Ken is in w,t, where he is perceiving a woman, Heather, walking across the street. Pointing at her, he says

(A) That woman is nice.

Ken expresses the proposition

(Aw) [[THAT$_{=h,J wt}$ W^*: x] [N^*x]]

(where THAT$_{=h,J wt}$ is the result of saturating the second and third argument places of the four-place relation expressed by 'that' with the properties of being identical to Heather and being jointly instantiated in w,t, respectively; W^* is the property of being a woman and N^* is the property of being nice). This proposition is true at an arbitrary world w'' iff being a woman and being identical to Heather are uniquely jointly instantiated in w,t in some object x, and x is nice at w''. Now imagine a world w' that is exactly like w in every way except that there is one more electron in the Andromeda galaxy in w' than there is in w (or at least w and w' are as much alike as is possible, given this difference). Since w and w' are alike in every other way, Ken in w' utters (A) in "exactly the same circumstance" looking at Heather walking across the street. Then Ken expresses the proposition:

(Aw') [[THAT$_{=h,\mathrm{J}w't}$ W^*: x] [N^*x]]
This proposition is true at an arbitrary world w'' iff being a woman and being identical to Heather are uniquely jointly instantiated in w',t in some object x, and x is nice at w''. Now (Aw) and (Aw') are *different* propositions (one requires that being a woman and being identical to Heather are uniquely jointly instantiated in w,t; the other requires that being a woman and being identical to Heather are uniquely jointly instantiated in w',t). But surely this is implausible! How could the presence of an extra electron in the Andromeda galaxy have the effect that John didn't say the same thing/express the same proposition in w and w'?

I think there are three points to be made in responding. First, I believe that our ordinary notion of "saying the same thing" is sufficiently loose that on virtually any plausible account of propositions, two people (or a person at one time and that same person at another, etc.) will correctly be said to have "said the same thing" when they utter sentences that express different propositions. E.g., in the ordinary sense of saying the same thing, if one of Chris's coworkers says to the boss 'There is something wrong with Chris today' and another later says to the boss 'Chris is acting oddly today', the boss might well correctly say to the second coworker 'Funny, someone else said the same thing' (fill in your own example if you don't like this one). Now assuming Heather is a woman at w,t and w',t, which of course we are, (Aw) and (Aw') will not diverge in truth value at any world. So, (given this assumption) they are necessarily equivalent. Further, intuitively both are "about" Heather (she is what uniquely jointly instantiates being identical to Heather and being a woman in both w,t and w',t) and both predicate the same property (being nice) of her. Finally, they have exactly the same structure and the same constituents except for one containing THAT$_{=h,\mathrm{J}w't}$ exactly where the other contains THAT$_{=h,\mathrm{J}wt}$. Now this really is a very tight, intimate connection between two propositions! Certainly, it is sufficiently tight to say, in the ordinary sense, that Ken said the same thing in w and w'.

But it was also claimed that it is *implausible* that Ken expressed two different propositions. Here, we are not dealing with an ordinary notion ("saying the same thing"), but a *technical*, *theoretical* notion: that of expressing different/or identical propositions. Surely there is no *ordinary* notion of expressing different propositions in the way that there is of saying the same thing. Different semantic theories will make different claims about the conditions under which two sentences (taken in contexts) express the same or different propositions. The fact that a theory claims that two sentences (in contexts) express different propositions and that this is *pretheoretically* implausible ought to be given little or no weight. For this is just a reflection of pretheoretical intuitions about a theoretical notion! And certainly, we don't want to hold theories accountable to pretheoretic intuitions about theoretical notions. Some *reason* must be given as to why a theory that claims that two sentences (in contexts) express different propositions is not a good theory. And none is currently on offer.

Finally, let me add that according to standard treatments of 'actual', if Ken says in both w and w' 'The actual inventor of skiing was Norwegian', where w and w' differ only in one electron in the Andromeda galaxy, he will have expressed different propositions. But here too, in the ordinary sense, Ken said the same thing in both worlds. (Try asking your nonphilosopher friends!) Further, before the development of standard semantic treatments of definite descriptions and 'actual', people probably would have found the claim that different propositions were expressed in w and w' implausible! This highlights the worth of plausibility judgments in such cases.

29
I am not claiming that we couldn't, by adding a lot of background by way of stage setting, describe a case in which 'I wish I could ski like the man' would be passable even looking down on a ski run filled with male skiers. But notice that no stage setting is required at all for the use of the 'that' phrase to be felicitous. Thus, the 'that' phrase and the description behave differently, and that is all I need to claim here.

30
It is important to appreciate that if my intentions are not redundant in an NDNS use, then the property my intentions determine is semantically significant and affects which proposition I express *even if my audience doesn't recognize my intentions and the property they determine*. Of course, in such a case my audience won't know which proposition I express. In the example just given, if some of my friends weren't paying attention to the calculations being performed and don't know what we are working on, then when I utter 'Even I could slam dunk at that place' they will not know what proposition I am expressing. Still (assuming my intentions were the same as in the original story), I have expressed the same proposition as I did in the original story. Thus, in NDNS uses in which a speaker has nonredundant intentions, one's audience won't know what proposition was expressed if they don't have access to the speaker's intentions. But, of course, the speaker still expressed it.

31
They still can occur, however. This is consistent with what was said earlier: that demonstrations in such cases serve to give the audience access to the nonredundant intentions of the speaker. Thus demonstrations are *required* when there is no other way to provide the audience access to the intentions of the speaker and the property they determine, and to make clear to the audience which occurrence of a 'that' phrase a given intention is associated with.

32
Recall that in QI uses the predicative material combined with the 'that' in a 'that' phrases contributes a *relation* to the proposition expressed, and the speaker's intention determines a relation as well (the *same* relation, if intentions are redundant).

33
I haven't specified the proposition expressed here, but have merely described the conditions under which it is true.

34
The data exhibited here and previously in arguing that in some NDNS and QI uses speaker intentions are not redundant seems to me to refute the claim that 'that' phrases in NDNS uses and QI uses are "stylistic variants" of definite descriptions. Presumably, in saying this, one means that the 'that' phrases in these uses are functioning semantically exactly as definite descriptions do. But if this were so, one would think that if a use in a sentence of 'that *F*' is felicitous (and a stylistic variant of 'the *F*'), substituting 'the *F*' for 'that *F*' would preserve felicity. However, as we have seen, in general felicity is not preserved under such substitutions in NDNS and QI uses of 'that' phrases. Of course, we take this latter fact to be evidence for the claim that the uses of 'that' phrases in question function semantically in a way *different* from definite descriptions (in allowing speakers' intentions to be relevant to their semantics). Obviously, the "stylistic variant" theorist must give some other account of this fact. Thanks to Mark Crimmins for a discussion of these issues.

35
NDNS uses could be rigid in unusual cases, because the property expressed by the predicative material in the 'that' phrase or the property determined by the speaker's intentions or the "conjunction" of these two properties might have as its extension the same thing in all possible worlds. If the reader imagines such cases, she will see that they are unusual. See also the discussion of the interaction of NDNS uses and modal operators in chapter 3 (examples (2) and (3) and the surrounding discussion) for addi-

tional evidence that (at least some) NDNS uses are not rigid. Again, I will consider the possibility that some (more usual) NDNS uses are rigid shortly.

36
I use 'pick out' because though rigid, the 'that' phrase, of course, is not a referring expression on the present view.

37
Thanks to an anonymous referee for raising issues that led to my thinking about these various versions of my account just discussed.

38
The issue of whether the view I have formulated might be formulated in this other way was raised by Jason Stanley, whom I thank for his comments on this matter.

Chapter Three

1
In discussing the scope interaction between negation and 'that' phrases, we shall also briefly consider how 'that' phrases interact with what are usually called *monotone decreasing* quantifiers.

2
In saying this, I assume that 'that' quantifiers, like other quantifiers, range over the domain of the world where they are being evaluated.

3
NDNS cases of the sort we shall consider except that speaker intentions are *not* redundant differ only in having an additional property (determined by the speaker's intentions) restrict the quantification expressed by the 'that' phrase. Thus from the standpoint of interaction with modal operators, such uses are not interestingly different from those we shall consider, but are somewhat more complex to describe.

4
Again, I use the 'should have been' in (2) to suppress the epistemic reading of 'It is possible' and make the metaphysical reading more salient.

5
An anonymous referee agreed that we can make sense of (2) as in some way characterizing a counterfactual situation in which a plant other than the one that was actually picked last had the property of being picked last and was type A. But he or she didn't think this reading of (2) results from the 'that' phrase in (2) taking narrow scope with respect to the modal operator. He or she noted

that in the sentence (from Geoff Nunberg), 'You shouldn't open the door without looking—I might have been a thief', 'I might have been a thief', has a reading where it characterizes a counterfactual situation in which someone other than the speaker is a thief and appears at the door at the time the speaker did (as opposed to the reading that characterizes a counterfactual situation in which the speaker is a thief). Let us call this the N *reading*. This reading presumably has nothing to do with scope (since 'I' doesn't have variable scope). But then the referee thought that perhaps whatever (nonscopal) mechanism produces the N reading of Nunberg's example could produce a reading of (2) on which it characterizes a counterfactual situation in which a plant other than the one that was actually picked last had the property of being picked last and was type A. Thus, he or she thought that the fact that (2) has a reading of the sort mentioned doesn't show that the 'that' phrase in it takes narrow scope with respect to the modal operator. However, note that there are ways of suppressing the N reading of Nunberg's example. Suppose I say: 'The world could have been different in many ways. For example, I could have been a thief instead of a professor'. Surely it is very hard to get the N reading of the second sentence here. Clearly, the natural reading is the one on which the counterfactual situation being considered is one in which I am a thief! But now consider 'The world could have been different in many ways. For example, that last plant you pulled from plot two could have been of type A instead of type B'. We would expect the N reading to be suppressed here too, since the example is exactly like the one just considered. But the final sentence here is naturally read as characterizing a counterfactual situation in which a plant other than the one that was actually picked last had the property of being picked last and was type A. So this reading cannot be the N reading, since it ought to be suppressed here. Thus, it must result from the 'that' phrase taking narrow scope with respect to the modal operator, contrary to what was suggested by the referee. See also the next note.

6

We can also get examples in which NDNS uses take narrow scope with respect to temporal operators. So for example, suppose I know on general grounds that there is exactly one Provost of Student Affairs and that he is a male. I also know that his term as Provost is up next year. This position has come up in discussions of various university administrative positions, and noting the small number of females in such posts and the pressure to have more in them, but with no particular female in mind, I say: 'Next year that Provost will be a woman'. Here we get the narrow scope reading of the 'that' phrase relative to the temporal operator. Note that it is very hard to get N readings (see previous note) of tensed examples such as this. If the current male Provost says: 'Next year, I will be a woman', it is extremely hard for this to be read as asserting that someone other than he will occupy his position and be female next year. So attempting to explain what appears to be a narrow scope reading of the 'that' phrase relative to a temporal operator by invoking N readings seems hopeless here. I should also mention that the fact that (2) and (3) have true readings where NDNS uses of 'that' phrases take narrow scope with respect to modal operators (and in so doing must pick out different individuals in different circumstances of evaluation) again shows that (at least some) NDNS uses are nonrigid.

7
As in the NDNS uses just considered, I shall assume the speaker's intentions are redundant in the QI uses that follow. For again, not making that assumption here merely adds gratuitous complexity.

8
The reading on which the 'that' phrase takes wide scope over the modal operator would be true in the actual world iff every professor in the actual world cherished in some possible world w' what is his or her first publication in the actual world. It is very hard to get this reading of the sentence. See the next paragraph.

9
On this reading, the sentence would claim that every man x and some woman x kissed y are such that it is possible that x loves y. The truth of this proposition at a world w' would require every man x at w' and some woman x kissed at w' y to be such that in some world w'' x loves y. Note that x need not have kissed y at w''.

10
Thanks to Zoltan Gendler Szabo for helping me to see this.

11
And, indeed, it is hard to read other quantifiers as taking narrow scope in similar constructions. Thus in:

Some student is not bald

Every student is not bald

Most students are not bald

it is difficult to read the quantifiers as taking narrow scope with respect to negation. However, there still seem to be differences between how these quantifiers interact with negation and how definite descriptions and 'that' phrases do. See the next note.

12

Assuming, of course, that the evidence we have for thinking that 'that' phrases are quantificational is comparable to the evidence we have for thinking that definite descriptions are quantificational. Much of the present work can be construed as attempting to show just this. An anonymous referee appeared to miss this point when he or she noted that there doesn't appear to be a reading of 'That man with a purple hat did not marry my sister' on which it "asserts the nonexistence of a purple-hatted sister-marrying man." (I assume he or she was imagining an NDNS use of the 'that' phrase, since the example was given in the discussion of such cases.) But to the extent that it is hard to get such a reading of the sentence here, it is equally hard to read 'The man with a purple hat did not marry my sister' as asserting the non-existence of a purple-hatted sister-marrying man. So, just as I claimed, definite descriptions and 'that' phrases behave in similar ways here. There is a further interesting phenomenon involving the interaction of negation and quantifiers. In general, expressing negation in the form of the sentence operator 'It is not the case that ...' placed in front of a quantified sentence results in negation taking wide scope over the quantifiers in the sentence. Thus the following sentences are all naturally read this way:

It is not the case that every student is happy.

It is not the case that some student is happy.

It is not the case that few/many students are happy.

However, when we try this with definite descriptions, the result is different:

It is not the case that the present King of France is happy.

Here, this just seems to be a variant of

The present King of France is not happy,

which is read most naturally with the description taking wide scope over negation. Similarly,

It is not the case that that person who climbed El Capitan is happy

is most naturally read with the 'that' phrase taking wide scope over negation. Why definite descriptions and 'that' phrases differ form other quantifiers in this respect is not entirely clear.

13

With the data discussed earlier, this suggests to me that there is a strong tendency for quantifiers to take wide scope over sentence-internal negation.

14

It *may* be that D results from (15) having the reading (15c) *and* the (alleged) fact that the use of a definite description triggers something like a presupposition that the description is satisfied. Though something like this seems plausible to me, I don't attempt to resolve such issues here, as they are irrelevant to my main concerns.

15

I am again assuming here that 'that' phrases (or rather their propositional contributions) qua quantifiers range over the domain of the world at which they are evaluated. So in (17a)/(17b) they attempt to find some individual *in w'* that is identical to b and has F^* *in w,t*. If there is no such individual in w' (either because b doesn't exist there or because it isn't F^* in w,t), (17b) is true and (17a) is false.

16

In discussing competing quantificational accounts of 'that' phrases in chapter 2, I imagined a defender of what I there called T_1 telling a story similar to the one I just told here as to why 'that' phrases don't take narrow scope with respect to modal operators. In rejecting T_1, I criticized this explanation. My point there was that if a story of the sort just told is a *pragmatic* explanation of why certain readings are suppressed, presumably these pragmatic considerations can be overridden in certain cases allowing the suppressed reading to come through. And in the case discussed by the T_1 defender, my claim was that the reading in question *never* arises. Here, I am claiming that a certain mechanism, in conjunction with others, strongly suppresses readings corresponding to (17b). However, I claim that such readings *do* arise in extreme cases. Thus my criticism of the T_1 theorist in chapter 2 is not in conflict with what I say here.

17

To avoid certain subtle complications, suppose the facial features, etc., were completely computer generated, and so are not those of any real man who has ever or will ever exist.

18

Note that even if one denies that my intention has an object in such a case, this won't make the reading corresponding to (17a) true. For (17a)'s truth requires there to be a unique instance x of being a man and something else in w,t, and requires that thing not to exist. Thus, it appears that the reading of (19) corresponding to (17a) would never be true in the context in which it was uttered. Further, if, as we are supposing, a quantifier when evaluated at a world and time ranges over the individuals existing at that world and time, the reading of (19) corresponding to (17a) cannot be true at any world. For this proposition to be true at a world w' would require b to exist at w' (and be a man at w,t), so that the quantifier could range over it, and would require b not to exist at w', so as to satisfy the portion of the proposition other than the quantifier. One other point: suppose that as my audience is looking at the hologram and before I tell them it is a hologram, I say, pointing at it, 'No person who works here has ever had lunch with that man'. I then add 'because that man doesn't exist'. It seems that the first sentence has a true reading here. But, as in the cases involving 'that' phrases and monotone decreasing quantifiers discussed when we considered NDNS uses and negation, the only true reading of the sentence would result from the 'that' phrase taking narrow scope with respect to the monotone decreasing quantifier 'No person who works here'. For only this reading can be true if b (the hologram) isn't a man. So here again, we have a 'that' phrase taking narrow scope with respect to another scoped element.

19

That b not be a boulder is sufficient for the truth of (21b), and there is a sense in which if it isn't a boulder but some other heavy object (steel painted as a boulder) and *is* floating in air unsupported, I am wrong. Nonetheless (21b) would be true in such a case. Presumably, what I am wrong about, as the situation was described, is my background belief to the effect that heavy things can't hang unsupported in air.

20

It is very easy to get what we take to be wide scope readings of 'that' phrases relative to verbs of propositional attitude. These are the readings that the direct reference theorists claim result from 'that' phrases directly referring. So all parties agree these readings are present (though, of course, there is a dispute concerning how they arise). Thus, such readings are of limited interest to us.

21

Again, because nonredundant intentions introduce pointless complexity, I here and below continue to assume intentions are redundant.

22

That Scott does not believe a singular proposition in such a case was defended in chapter 1. See the discussion of the NDNS use involving Greg and the math exam. I am assuming here that Scott, like Greg in chapter 1, never introduced a directly referential expression whose reference is fixed by a uniquely satisfied description he has at his disposal (here 'the hominid who discovered how to start fires').

23

Thanks to Mark Crimmins for helpful discussion of examples similar to some I use here. Looking back at (25a) and (25b), it should be clear that so long as Alan is the guy who was named CEO of Chanticleer in w,t (the context of utterance), if (25b) is true, so is (25a). If Sherry believes that being identical to b (Alan) and being a guy just named CEO of Chanticleer have a unique instance x and x hates her, then Sherry believes of b, who is the guy who has just been named CEO of Chanticleer, that he hates her. Since if the narrow scope readings are true in such cases, so are the wide scope readings, we cannot simply appeal to the fact that ascriptions seem true to defend the claim that there are narrow scope readings in these cases. For an opponent could claim that the intuition about truth in such a case arises from the *wide scope* reading (or a reading that is equivalent, or nearly equivalent to the wide scope reading—e.g., a reading arising because the 'that' phrase is claimed to be directly referential). Since appeal to simple intuitions about truth of ascriptions wouldn't supply us with evidence of narrow scope readings in these cases, we have had to, e.g., consider whether (25) in the described situation *explains* Sherry's behavior; consider intuitions about *falsity* of certain belief ascriptions; and consider cases in which it seems true to say 'John said that that F is G', even when the thing one intends to talk about by means of the 'that' phrase is not F.

Chapter Four

1

Whether they do or not is unimportant. What is important is that most theorists agree that there are cases in which nothing can be identified as the demonstrated or intended object.

2

See the appendix for a proof that 'that' satisfies CIC. It should be clear that it won't satisfy CAC. Consider the propositions expressed by utterances of 'That A is B' and 'That A is BA' in w,t by someone whose perceptual intention has b as its object. In such a case, these sentences express the following propositions, respectively:

(i) $[[\text{THAT}_{=b,Jwt}\ A^*: x]\ [B^*\ x]]$

(ii) $[[\text{THAT}_{=b,Jwt}\ A^*: x]\ [B^*\ x\ \&\ A^*\ x]]$

Clearly (i) could be true at a world w' where (ii) is false. Just suppose b is A^* in w,t but not w', and is B^* at w'.

3

Within the framework of the sort I am employing, this is an informal description of a notion that is closely related to what is usually called *permutation invariance* in the generalized quantifier literature. See, e.g., Keenan and Westerstahl (1997). In what follows I somewhat more precisely, but still loosely, sketch this relative of permutation invariance within our framework. Thanks to Zoltan Gendler Szabo for suggesting I discuss these issues.

4

I say 'loosely' here because I have not sketched the ideas with the precision with which permutation invariance, and hence logicality, is characterized by, e.g., Keenan and Westerstahl (1997). More importantly, the relevant notions are not characterized in works such as this within a framework that includes properties (rather than sets), propositions, and possible worlds. Thus the resulting notions are different but related.

It is worth noting that an f-permutation of a given possible world w need not be a metaphysically possible world. For f may assign extensions to properties and relations such that it is not metaphysically possible for members of the extensions to possess those properties and relations, (e.g., f could map things in the extension of the property of being human at w to inanimate objects that presumably could not have been human). We could avoid appeal to worlds that aren't metaphysically possible by defining, for a (metaphysically possible) world w, the f-extension of properties and relations in w (where f is a one-one function from the domain of w onto the domain of w and the f-extension of a property/relation may include things that can't instantiate/ stand in the property/relation). We could then define f-truth in w for propositions, where the definition of f-truth appeals to the f-extensions, rather than the extensions, of properties and relations in w. Finally, we could characterize logicality in terms of the proposition expressed by a sentence containing a determiner being true at w iff for all f, it is f-true at w. To do all this would be a bit more tedious and cumbersome than appealing to metaphysically impossible worlds. Since the appeal is eliminable, I make it.

5

See Keenan and Stavi (1986) and Keenan and Westerstahl (1997).

6

Conversations with Jason Stanley and Zoltan Gendler Szabo helped me clarify my thinking on this matter. I borrow the phrase 'quantifier domain restriction' from them.

7
Bach (1994) defends a theory of this sort.

8
Stanley and Szabo (2000) is a view of this sort.

9
For the remainder of my discussion of the present issue, I ignore the properties of being jointly instantiated and being jointly instantiated in w,t (where w,t are the world and time of the context of utterance). Bringing these properties in would add a lot of complexity and my point can be made without them.

10
E.g., Stanley and Szabo (2000) hold that it is the semantic value of the N$'$ constituent of a quantifier phrase that varies with context.

11
E.g., Stanley and Szabo (2000) discuss an approach they call the *metalinguistic semantic parameter approach*.

12
Note that on a view of quantifier domain restriction according to which, e.g., in uttering (3) I *pragmatically convey* the proposition that every student in a particular class passed the exam, this phenomenon is clearly distinct from the phenomenon of 'that' phrases allowing supplementation by speakers' intentions. For the latter is a *semantic* phenomenon. This is what I meant earlier when I said that if the phenomena of quantifier domain restriction is a pragmatic phenomena, the worry under discussion does not arise.

13
Perhaps sentences like (4) have another reading on which 'one' can be read as having as its semantic value the property of being a bottle in a collection of bottles other than that "picked out" by its antecedent. If it does have such a reading, 'one' behaves like a pronoun of laziness in such a case. I find such alleged readings somewhat hard to get. But in any case, whether there are such readings doesn't matter for present purposes. I claim only that the reading of (4) according to which 'one' gets its semantic value from its antecedent 'bottles', so that the second conjunct of (4) is "about" the same group of bottles as the first, is the most natural reading of the sentence here. Indeed, I only need to claim that the sentence *can* be read this way.

Finally, some may object that the anaphor 'one' is not an N$'$ anaphor in (4) and the other examples I consider, since its antecedent appears to be an *NP* (in (4) 'every bottle') and it seems to occupy the syntactic position of an NP. So far as I can see, nothing hangs on whether 'one' is an N′ anaphor in the examples I consider. The important point is that the sentences I consider have readings on which what 'one' ranges over is determined by the semantic value in the context in question of the N′ that is, or is a constituent of, its antecedent. To highlight this fact, I call 'one' an N′ anaphor in these sentences.

14
Conversations with Jason Stanley regarding his and Szabo's account of quantifier domain restriction suggested to me that considering cases of N′ ellipsis might be useful here. Again, I need not claim that the second conjunct of (10) *can't* be read as being "about" a different group of bottles than the first. I claim only that the reading on which both conjuncts are "about" the same group of bottles is the most natural reading. And again, I really only need the weaker claim that the sentence can be read this way.

15
I use 'implication' in a broad, unanalyzed sense here that doesn't require the implications in question to have the same source or character. In particular, it allows that, for example, one implication may be semantic and the other may be pragmatic.

16
In talking about the lack of *conflict* here, as with 'implication', I am using 'conflict' broadly so that, e.g., if definite descriptions *semantically* require unique satisfaction and the use of 'some *F*' *pragmatically* conveys that there is more than one *F*, the two conjuncts in a sentence like 'The *F* is *G* and some *F* is *H*' would conflict. See the previous note.

17
Of course, my discussion here assumes that quantifier domain restriction is a semantic phenomenon (though, again, I should not be taken to be endorsing such a view). For as I said, if it is merely pragmatic, then this phenomenon is clearly distinct from the *semantic* phenomenon of 'that' allowing supplementation by speakers' intentions. And in any case, the data we have lately considered strongly suggest that quantifier domain restriction and supplementation by speakers' intentions of 'that' phrases, *however each is understood*, are different phenomena. One complex issue I leave unresolved here is whether it can be shown that 'that' phrases can simultaneously undergo both "ordinary" quantifier domain restriction (whereby the semantic value of its N′ constituent is affected) and the sort of supplementation whereby the semantic value of the determiner 'that' is affected.

18
Thanks to two anonymous referees who suggested I address this issue. Though I have discussed only 'that' phrases, I do suppose that the account I have sketched here is to be extended to other complex demonstratives, such as 'this *F*', 'these *Fs*', and 'those *Fs*'. Some have claimed that the account I have sketched cannot be extended to, e.g., 'this' phrases (and presumably 'these' phrases), because such phrases do not exhibit NDNS or QI uses. But this claim is simply incorrect. Suppose that I know on general grounds that exactly one skier from Truckee (I don't know who) skied the peak called 'Meteorite' in Alaska. We are in Alaska looking up at Meteorite and Tracy says that nobody could ski that peak. I respond: 'Well, this skier from Truckee skied it several years ago'. My use of the 'this' phrase is an NDNS use here. Further, suppose in explaining why I like NBA basketball, I say to my friend 'Every NBA game has this moment in it when two very talented teams struggle for control of the game'. Here we have a QI use of a 'this' phrase. Of course, *some* "attempted" QI uses of 'this' phrases sound terrible. My suspicion is that, among other things, this results from the "perspectival" meaning/connotation of 'this'. Similar remarks apply to 'these' phrases.

19
Of course current syntactic theory already posits null or empty constituents of various sorts, so positing one here is not at all a radical move.

20
Thus this third view is really a version of the first, where the contribution of the empty N' constituent is determined by context. But in this specific version (where I have specified the mechanism whereby the contribution of the N' constituent is determined) it is always the property that is determined by the speaker's intentions and saturates the second argument place in the four-place relation expressed by 'that'. Obviously, other versions of the first approach would not work in this way.

21
Though as my remarks below suggest, all the options scouted could provide some explanation why 'that' qua determiner can occur alone. Of course, sometimes other determiners can occur without overt N' constituents, as in 'Many try, few succeed'. But there is always the feeling that there is a missing N' constituent *with a specific content* (e.g., 'people', or perhaps some more specific predicate, depending on the context of utterance). Not so with simple 'that'. Thus, if I were to extend my account to handle simple 'that', and so treat it is a determiner, it would be, qua determiner, unique in this respect.

22

Of course, the means by which the quantification is restricted in the two cases differ. The property determined by the speaker's intention in a context partly determines what the *determiner* 'that' contributes to the proposition expressed in that context. Not so, of course, for the property expressed by the N′ constituent that is combined with the determiner.

Chapter Five

1

A number of people have raised something like the objection I am about to consider, including David Braun, David Kaplan, Ernie Lepore, Robert May, and Terence Parsons. However, I do not wish to attribute the precise objection I discuss to any of them.

2

An anonymous referee recommended an alternative strategy for the direct reference theorist. Instead of claiming that 'that' phrases are ambiguous, with one semantic account being required for certain uses and another for other uses, the direct reference theorist could try to (in his or her words) "refine the identifying criteria for being a genuine complex demonstrative" (appealing to phonological properties; the presence of a demonstration; or what have you) and then claim that uses the direct reference account can't handle (NDNS uses; QI uses; or whatever) don't meet these criteria and so aren't genuine complex demonstratives. The referee's idea was that strictly this may not be an ambiguity account, since on this view there is no *single* category of expression (e.g., complex demonstrative) for which two different semantic accounts are given. Perhaps this is so, but the view still posits two different semantic treatments for (what are orthographically) 'that' phrases. And I believe that the considerations raised in the present chapter suggest that an account that provides a unified semantics for 'that' phrases (or at least the uses considered in the present work) is superior to an account that posits two different semantic accounts for 'that' phrases, whether *strictly* an ambiguity account or not.

3

Of course, the rigidifying effect in a 'that' phrase *could* come from overt linguistic material in the phrase as well. Thus we could have an NDNS use containing the word 'actual' or a nominal expressing a uniquely satisfied property whose extension is constant across possible worlds. The point is that *in general* the rigidity of some uses of 'that' phrases is not traceable to overt linguistic material.

4
Excepting unusual cases, such as using the word 'actual' in an NDNS use of a 'that' phrase.

5
Brian Weatherson noted that adding 'but not that one' makes (2) smoother.

6
Some who agree that one can't *easily* get the anaphoric reading in (3″) claim that they can get it, though it is very strained. By contrast they claim that one simply cannot get the reading at all in the case of (3). These same people find they can get the anaphoric reading, though again it is very strained, in the case of (3b). But they agree that the anaphoric reading is much easier to get in (3′) than in either (3b) or (3″). Here, as elsewhere, I will be happy enough if 'that' phrases behave as definite descriptions do, since most agree that definite descriptions are quantifiers. So the crucial point here is that 'that' phrases *do* behave as definite descriptions do and both behave differently from names/referring expressions (in the sense that all agree that it is easier to get the anaphoric reading in the case of (3′) than it is in the case of both (3″) and (3b)).

Appendix

1
Note that a closed *formula* may express a *propositional frame* with free variables, as a result of $f(c)$ containing free variables that are not bound in the propositional frame. Though the formalism allows this, such cases are of no intuitive interest as far as I can see.

2
Two comments on this. First, this would have to be complicated if we wanted to have sentences containing distinct occurrences of 'that', where we want different speaker intentions to be associated with the different occurrences. We would have to have f map c to a sequence of propositional frames, and have h map c to a sequence of the same length, each element of which is the property of being jointly instantiated or being jointly instantiated in w,t (where w,t are the world and time of the context in question) depending on the corresponding element in the sequence f maps c to. The current formulation in effect amounts to unrealistically requiring distinct occurrences of 'that' in a sentence to be associated with the same intention. Second, in having $f(c)$ be a propositional frame instead of a property or relation, we avoid

complication by solving a certain problem trivially. As I have indicated, in the case of QI uses, the speaker's intentions must not only determine a relation, but must distinguish between its argument places in a certain way (in the discussion of (8) in chapter 2, I said that the speaker's intention had to distinguish between the argument places in: y is x's first black diamond run attempted, because in using the 'that' phrase, the speaker intuitively intends to talk about the first black diamond run attempted y for most avid skiers x). By making $f(c)$ a propositional frame, we distinguish different argument places by different occurrences of variables, which will end up being bound by different "quantifier contributions" in the proposition.

3
Nothing should be read into the fact that I define truth for propositions with respect to worlds *and times*. In particular, this should not be taken as indicating that I think of real propositions as entities that change truth value over time.

References

Bach, Kent. 1994. "Conversational Impliciture." *Mind and Language* 9: 124–162.

Braun, David. 1994. "Structured Characters and Complex Demonstratives." *Philosophical Studies* 74: 193–219.

Braun, David. 1996. "Demonstratives and Their Linguistic Meanings." *Noûs* 30: 145–173.

Chomsky, Noam. 1981. *Lectures on Government and Binding.* Dordrecht: Foris Publications.

Chomsky, Noam. 1982. *Some Concepts and Consequences of the Theory of Government and Binding.* Cambridge, Mass.: MIT Press.

Higginbotham, James and Robert May. 1981. "Crossing, Markedness, Pragmatics." In A. Belletti, L. Brandi, and L. Rizzi (eds.), *Theory of Markedness in Generative Grammar.* Pisa: Scuola Normales Superiore, 423–444.

Hornstein, Norbert. 1995. *Logical Form: From GB to Minimalism.* Cambridge, Mass.: Blackwell Publishers.

Kaplan, David. 1977. "Demonstratives." In J. Almog, J. Perry, and H. Wettstein (eds.), *Themes from Kaplan.* New York/Oxford: Oxford University Press, 1989, 481–563.

Kaplan, David. 1989. "Afterthoughts." In J. Almog, J. Perry, and H. Wettstein (eds.), *Themes from Kaplan.* New York/Oxford: Oxford University Press, 1989, 565–614.

Keenan, E. and J. Stavi. 1986. "A Semantic Characterization of Natural Language Determiners." *Linguistics and Philosophy* 9: 253–326.

Keenan, E. L. and D. Westerstahl. 1997. "Generalized Quantifiers in Linguistics and Logic." In J. van Benthem and A. ter Meulen (eds.), *Handbook of Logic and Language*. Cambridge, Mass.: MIT Press, 837–893.

King, Jeffrey C. 1994. "Can Propositions be Naturalistically Acceptable?" In P. French, T. Uehling, and H. Wettstein (eds.), *Midwest Studies in Philosophy XIX*. Notre Dame, Indiana: University of Notre Dame Press, 53–75.

King, Jeffrey C. 1995. "Structured Propositions and Complex Predicates." *Noûs* 29: 516–535.

King, Jeffrey C. 1996. "Structured Propositions and Sentence Structure." *Journal of Philosophical Logic* 25: 496–521.

King, Jeffrey C. 1999. "Are Complex 'That' Phrases Devices of Direct Reference?" *Noûs* 33: 155–182.

Kripke, Saul. 1980. *Naming and Necessity*. Cambridge, Mass.: Harvard University Press.

Larson, Richard and Peter Ludlow. 1993. "Interpreted Logical Forms." *Synthese* 95: 305–355.

Lepore, Ernest and Kirk Ludwig. 2000. "The Semantics and Pragmatics of Complex Demonstratives." *Mind* 109: 199–240.

May, Robert. 1985. *Logical Form: Its Structure and Derivation*. Cambridge, Mass.: MIT Press.

Neale, Stephen. 1990. *Descriptions*. Cambridge, Mass.: MIT Press.

Neale, Stephen. 1993. "Term Limits." In J. Tomberlin (ed.), *Philosophical Perspectives, 7: Logic and Language*. Atascadero, California: Ridgeview Publishing, 89–123.

Richard, Mark. 1993. "Articulated Terms." In J. Tomberlin (ed.), *Philosophical Perspectives, 7: Logic and Language*. Atascadero, California: Ridgeview Publishing, 207–230.

Stanley, Jason and Zoltan Gendler Szabo. 2000. "On Quantifier Domain Restriction." *Mind and Language* 15: 219–261.

Index

'Actual', 147–148, 185 (n.28), 198 (n.3)
Anaphora. *See* Bach-Peters sentences; Weak crossover phenomena
Antecedent contained deletion. *See* Verb phrase (VP) deletion

Bach, K., 195 (n.7)
Bach-Peters sentences, 12–15, 20, 140
Belief ascriptions. *See* Verbs of propositional attitude
Braun, D., 65–66, 172 (n.5), 183 (n.28)

C-command, 17–18, 157, 175 (nn.14–15). *See also* Verb phrase (VP) deletion
Character
  demonstrations and, 28, 172 (n.3)
  in a quantificational account, 84–85
  reference failure and, 117
  role of predicative material in determining, 13–15, 19–21
Chomsky, N., 174 (n.12)
Classic demonstrative uses of 'that' phrases, 2, 29, 51–52
  demonstrations and, 73

modal operators and, 88–89
movement and, 156–159
negation and, 103–109
quantifier domain restriction and, 126–139
supplementation and, 150–151
used in comparing T1 and T2, 56–66
verbs of propositional attitude and, 110–116
Complex 'that' phrases. *See* 'That' phrases

Definite descriptions. *See* 'That' phrases, definite descriptions compared with
Demonstrations, 27–28, 32–33, 67–77, 150–151, 157, 179 (n.9)
Determiners. *See also* Quantifiers
  combine with N′ expressions, 24–25
  conservative, 119–121
  logical, 123–126
  monotone decreasing, 97–99, 191–192
  'no', 97–99, 191 (n.18)
  permutation invariant, 194 (nn.3–4)

Determiners (cont.)
  propositional contribution of, 24–26, 53, 119
  syntactically simple vs. complex, 124–126
Direct Reference. *See* 'That' phrases, direct reference account of

Hornstein, N., 175 (n.16)

Kaplan, D., 1, 38, 171 (n.1), 172 (n.5), 179 (n.9)
Keenan, E., 194 (nn. 3–5)
King, J., 171 (n.1), 176 (n.1), 177 (n.4), 180 (n.11, nn.14–16), 183 (n.28)
Kripke, S., 182 (n.25)

Larson, R., 175 (n.16)
Lepore, E., 178 (n.6), 182 (n.25)
Logical Form (LF), 16–18, 128, 156–157, 173 (n.9). *See also* Surface-structure (S-structure)
Ludlow, P., 175 (n.16)
Ludwig, K., 178 (n.6), 182 (n.25)

May, R., 174 (nn.12–13), 175 (n.16), 176 (n.17)
Modal operators. *See also* 'Actual'; 'Should have been'
  classic demonstrative uses and, 88–89
  NDNS uses and, 89–93
  QI uses and, 93–94
Movement
  names and, 18, 175 (n.16)
  quantifier, 16–18, 156–159, 161, 173 (n.9)
  referring expressions and, 156
Movement tests. *See* Verb phrase (VP) deletion; Weak crossover phenomena

Names
  compared with 'that' phrases, 7–8
  movement and, 18, 175 (n.16)
  treated as a quantifiers, 26–27
  weak crossover phenomena and, 18–19, 158–159
N′ constituents. *See also* Quantifier domain restriction
  combining with determiners, 24–25
  empty (or null), 141–145
  N′ anaphora, 129–135
  N′ ellipses, 135–139
NDNS (no demonstration, no speaker reference) uses of 'that' phrases, 2–3, 11
  Bach-Peters sentences and, 19–20
  character and, 19–20, 172 (n.3), 174 (n.10)
  modal operators and, 89–93
  negation and, 94–96, 98–100, 191 (n.18)
  nonredundant intentions and, 66–74, 151, 186 (n.34), 187 (n.3)
  nonrigid, 9–10, 39–40, 78, 82, 84, 149, 198 (n.2)
  quantifier domain restriction and, 131–139
  redundant intentions and, 54
  rigid, 82, 84, 186 (n.35), 198 (n.3), 199 (n.4)
  temporal operators and, 188 (n.6)
  used in comparing T1 and T2, 48–50, 52, 66–74
  verbs of propositional attitude and, 3–9, 110, 192 (n.22).
Neale, S., 27, 173 (n.8)
Negation
  classic demonstrative uses and, 103–109